SuperQuick™ Wordpress

Easy, FREE and Fast
Website, SMART PHONE and e-Commerce Solutions!

Wordpress is INCREDIBLY Powerful
and FREE software to quickly create an IMPRESSIVE
e-Commerce Presence on the Web
that works with SMART PHONES TOO.

This Book will show you how to
harness the power of Wordpress, step-by-step, with illustrations!

Learn the Mysteries of
Wordpress' FREE Shopping Carts, Free SEO,
and how to find and use Great Free Plugins, Widgets and More –

If you were trying to figure out how to *cost-effectively* get a Website and
SMART PHONE Solution –with e-Commerce and blogs –
here is your Answer - Revealed!

By M. Nicole van Dam

About the Cover Art: "Rat Race™" is a painting by M. Nicole van Dam.

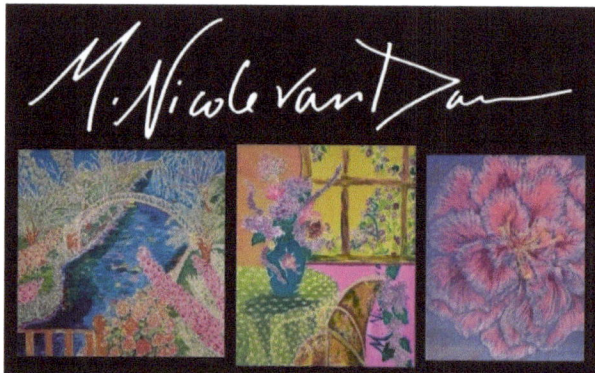

To see the artwork of the author and her own Wordpress site,
please visit **Nicole.Bz**.

How to Get a Business Website on the Web that works with Smart Phones too!

The way to use this book is to have it open on your lap while you work on Wordpress on your computer – this book is a step-by-step illustrated guide to Wordpress. This book walks you through setting up e-Commerce on Wordpress, as well as highlights lots of great other free software made for Wordpress.

Wordpress.org offers great FREE software that enables you to create FREE shopping carts and all other elements of a truly impressive, fully functional e-commerce website. By learning Wordpress you will free yourself of paying someone to work on your website, and you will open whole new doors of building community with your customers and selling successfully on the web. With Wordpress, you can create a website that combines e-Commerce with social media (even Facebook and Twitter). Wordpress even has an easy way for you to translate your Wordpress website so that it works on smart phones!

Learning Wordpress allows you to control your web-destiny, your smart-phone destiny, your social media and e-commerce destiny. The best part about Wordpress, other than its ease of use once you master it, is that **you get all the software you need to succeed <u>without paying for the software and without paying someone by the hour to develop your site</u>**. In other words, the powerful FREE software tools offered as part of the Wordpress community are why conquering Wordpress is worth the effort.

The Solution to your Business Website and Smart Phone Needs –
That is why this effort is worth doing.

Table of Contents

Prelude   page 6

Part 1 – Getting Started

Step 1 Choosing a Host   page 7

Step 2 Installing Wordpress   page 9

Step 3 Logging in to Wordpress   page 17

Part 2 – Working in Wordpress
Quick Steps to Creating Your Basic Wordpress Site

Step 4 – Choosing the 'Theme": Creating Your Basic Site Structure   page 20

Step 5 – Customizing the "Header" Image for your Site   page 24

Step 6 – Choosing & Customizing "Widgets" for Your Site   page 28

Step 7 - Customizing "Settings" ("Title" & User Comment Preferences)   page 38

Step 8 – Installing "Jetpack" Capabilities   page43

Step 9 – Setting up other important Wordpress "Dashboard" preferences   page 46

Part 3 - Adding e-Commerce

Step 10 – Installing the Ecwid Plugin   page 48

Step 11 – Adding a New Page to Your Wordpress Site   page 57

STEP 12 – Finishing Setting up the Store Back-End (Payment, Shipping, etc.) page 61

STEP 13 – Adding Your Own Products to the Store   page68

Part 4 – Posting to Your Wordpress Blog, Adding More Pages & Creating a Custom Menu below your Image Header

Step 14 - Posting to Your Wordpress Blog   page 80

Step 15 - Adding Pages to Your Wordpress Website
and Working with the "Pages" Widget   page 83

Step 16 – Creating Custom Menus Below Your Image Header   page 92

Part 5 Advanced Design, Plugins and Widgets Identifying and Using Key Plugins & Widgets

Step 17 - Visually Identifying Key Plugins & Widgets on a Website   page 95

Step 18 –   Identifying Behind-the-Scenes Plugins, for
Site Back-Up, SEO, Smart Phone Capability & More!   page 110

Part 6 - Appendix – Resizing Images in Adobe Photoshop   page 114

5

Prelude

We hope that this Book is of great use to You!

M. Nicole van Dam has been forging her own unique niche in the art world, and to do this she has had to conquer website design in a cost-effective way. Nicole wrote this book so that it would be easier for others to spend time on their Creative endeavors/field of choice, rather than on trying to demystify how to get a presence on the web.

To see the artwork of the author on her own Wordpress site, please visit Nicole.Bz.

Part 1
Getting Started

Step 1
The First Step is Choosing a Host - What You Need to Know

1. *There is a difference between Wordpress.com and Wordpress.org. Worpdress.com does NOT have the features we are talking about in this book. The Wordpress you want to use for this book is Wordpress.org.*

2. *Quick Background: Wordpress.org gives you, for free, their Wordpress software, for you to use on your site. The key is, you need to put that software (and your website) on a gadget that is connected 24x7 to the web – that gadget is called a "server."*

3. *You can get free access to a "server" if you don't wish to pay for a host – information regarding free hosting is also included in this book.*

4. *In other words, that free Wordpress software needs to be put, by you, onto a "server" that is connected to the web. Don't worry – this is not too hard to do – I will walk you through how I did it and it can be done in less than 30 minutes!*

5. *This book will show you how to get this free Wordpress.org software, how to choose a "host" to run that Wordpress software, and how to install the Wordpress software. While that may sound complicated, if you do exactly what I did, you can get it set up in less than 30 minutes, and you can even have someone on the phone walk you through it - not bad!*

6. *DETAIL ON YOUR SERVER CHOICES: You could put the software on YOUR own server. Don't have a server? Neither do I! -And I don't want the hassle of maintaining a server! -So I rented one, meaning that I pay an annual fee to a server "host" who keeps the server up and running and gives me great HUMAN customer service. What you need to know is that there are*

HUNDREDS of potential "hosts" out there - you can even find free hosts or you can pay hosts.

7. *FREE HOST: You can get free access to a server if you don't wish to pay for a host – as of the writing of this book, http://www.000webhost.com provides generous free hosting with 1500MB of free space and 100GB/month of data transfer, PHP 5 and MySQL, all free.*

8. *How I chose my host: I wanted to make sure I had solid customer service (when I call my host, every time (so far anyway!) I get a HUMAN BEING on the phone), so I opted to pay for my host. I found an inexpensive host that actually offers Wordpress as part of their own toolkit AND they have a real live human in their customer service department who can walk you through installing Wordpress on your site. As far as I'm concerned, that's perfect. All a long-winded way of saying, the host for my website that I pay is http://hypermart.net . As of the writing of this book, Hypermart has "hosting" plans for $4.25/month (and up). In case you're wondering, I don't have any ownership interest in Hypermart, and I don't get paid anything for saying I use them, and as I write this Hypermart doesn't even know I am working on this book.*

9. *Again, you don't need to use Hypermart as your host for your server. You could use your own server or you can use any host that has a server that can run Wordpress software. A free host, as of the writing of this book, is http://www.000webhost.com and according to their website they provide generous free hosting with 1500MB of free space and 100GB/month of data transfer, all free, with PHP 5 and MySQL also included free.*

10. *How do you know if a host can run Wordpress software? What you need to do is contact your prospective host and ASK them:*

    - *If I choose you as my host, can your server run the current version of Wordpress?*

    - *If the server host you are interviewing says they can run Wordpress, you should still double-check what they say by specifically asking them about the following two Wordpress requirements, which as of the writing of this*

8

book, are the Wordpress server requirements for Wordpress Version 3.2:

> ▪ *If I choose you as host, can your server run PHP version 5.2.4 or greater? If not, what version of PHP does your server run?*

> ▪ *If I choose you as host, can your server run MySQL version 5.0.15 or greater? If not, what version of MySQL does your server run?*

> ▪ *If I choose you as host, can your server support the mod_rewrite Apache module? (Note: This Apache module is not essential for the beginners like us)*

IMPORTANT NOTE ABOUT SERVER HOSTS: If you can't find a human being to talk to via phone to ask these basic questions, then they might not be the right host if you have problems down the line and like actually talking to people instead of waiting for email support.

As of the writing of this book, Wordpress Version 3.2 is the MOST recent version of the Wordpress software, but you can download and use an older version of Wordpress. I actually prefer an older version of Wordpress, because there are more free add-ons that work well with it. For me, I currently prefer Wordpress version 3.0.5, which works with hosts offering PHP 4.3 (or newer) and MySQL 4.1.2 (or newer)(these are easier requirements for hosts to satisfy too). You can find the current list of host server requirements for the version of Wordpress you choose at http://codex.wordpress.org/TemplateServer_requirements .

In addition, Wordpress has their own recommended list of hosts at http://wordpress.org/hosting and Wordpress gets a donation if someone uses one of those hosts. Also noteworthy: Wordpress offers their insights on hosting at http://codex.wordpress.org/Hosting_Wordpress

Step 2
Installing Wordpress

1. *This book walks you through, step-by-step with illustrations, installing Wordpress on http://hypermart.net – and I am using Hypermart as my example primarily because Hypermart is the actual host I use for my site, but also because if you get stuck Hypermart has a phone number you can call as a Hypermart client for free help: 877-287-5929 . Please know that Hypermart does not pay me to write this.*

2. *If you choose to use a host other than http://Hypermart.net (again, Hypermart is the host that I use but I am not employed by them in any sense), know that each host will have their own nuances of how to install Wordpress.*

3. **For those of you not using Hypermart as a host, Wordpress has done a good job of creating a detailed help page on installation, located at http://codex.wordpress.org.Installing_Wordpress. This Wordpress website page is where you will find Wordpress "Famous 5-Minute Install" instructions.**

4. *Assuming you use http://Hypermart.net, below is a screen capture of what you will see to sign up with Hypermart to start your Wordpress installation journey. The pink arrow below is drawn merely to point to the Wordpress icon on the Hypermart site. Please know that you can use a different host and still use Wordpress.org free software, that's entirely your call:*

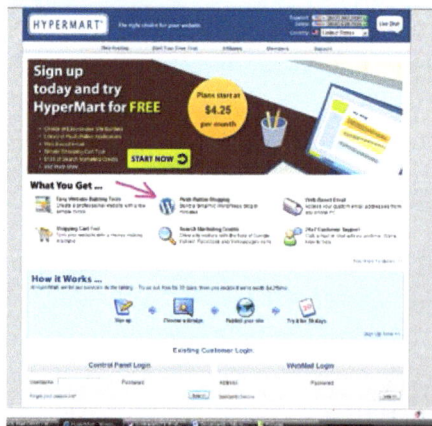

5.   *I like http://Hypermart.net because right up front in the top right corner of their site, http://Hypermart.net has a phone number you can call for support in installing Wordpress onto the http://Hypermart.net server – as of the date of this writing the Hypermart phone number is 877-287-5929. Every time I have called Hypermart, I reached a real human being without being charged extra for it, so if anything doesn't work for you during this process of installing Wordpress onto the Hypermart server, then you can call Hypermart – and they don't charge for the support call!*

6.   *—So if you were to sign up for Hypermart, you would first choose a username and password on the Hypermart site and give them your credit card, and then you will get to the Hypermart Control panel, shown below. You can see by the pink arrow how Wordpress is an automatic part of Hypermart's toolkit on their control panel.*

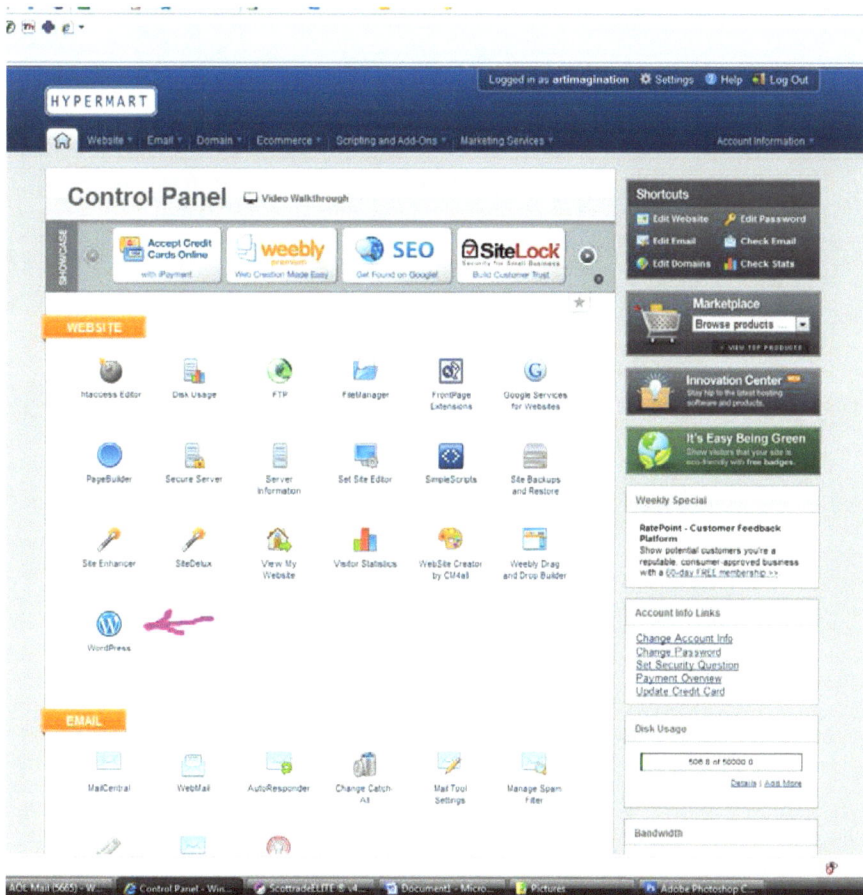

7. *INSTALLING WORDPRESS FROM HYPERMART CONTROL PANEL:*
    Locate the pink arrow I drew in below. As shown below, once at the
    Hypermart Control panel, click where the pink arrow is, on "SimpleScripts"
    which is the Hypermart installer for the free Wordpress software:

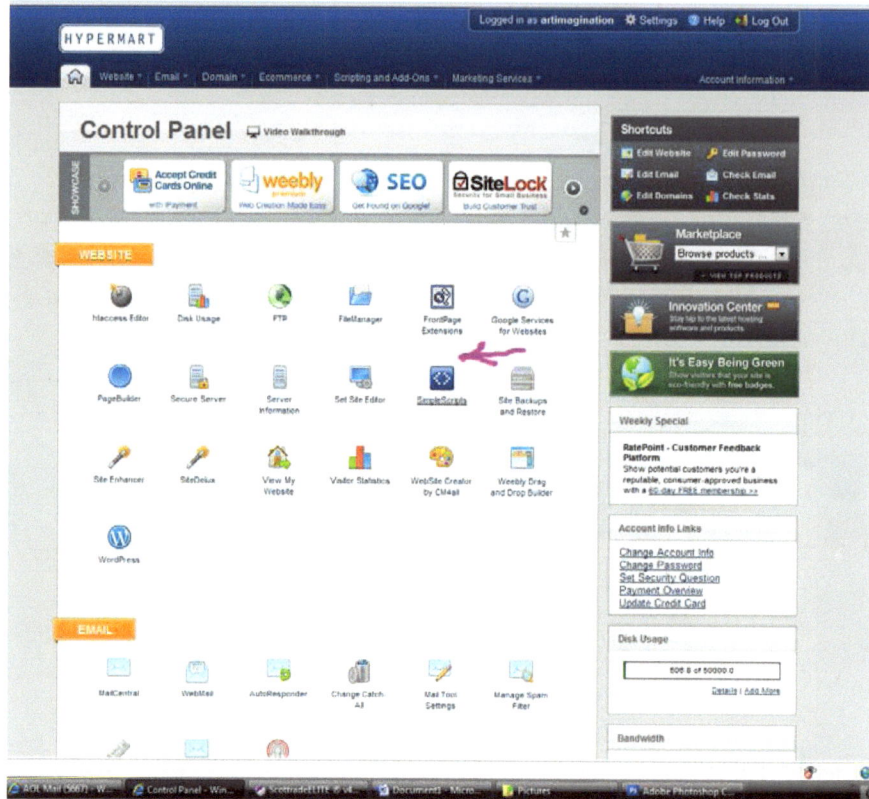

8. *Once you click "SimpleScripts" as shown in the previous step, this brings you to the screenshot below. Note that we are still working within the Hypermart control panel environment. Now you should click the "Wordpress" icon, shown where the pink arrow is below:*

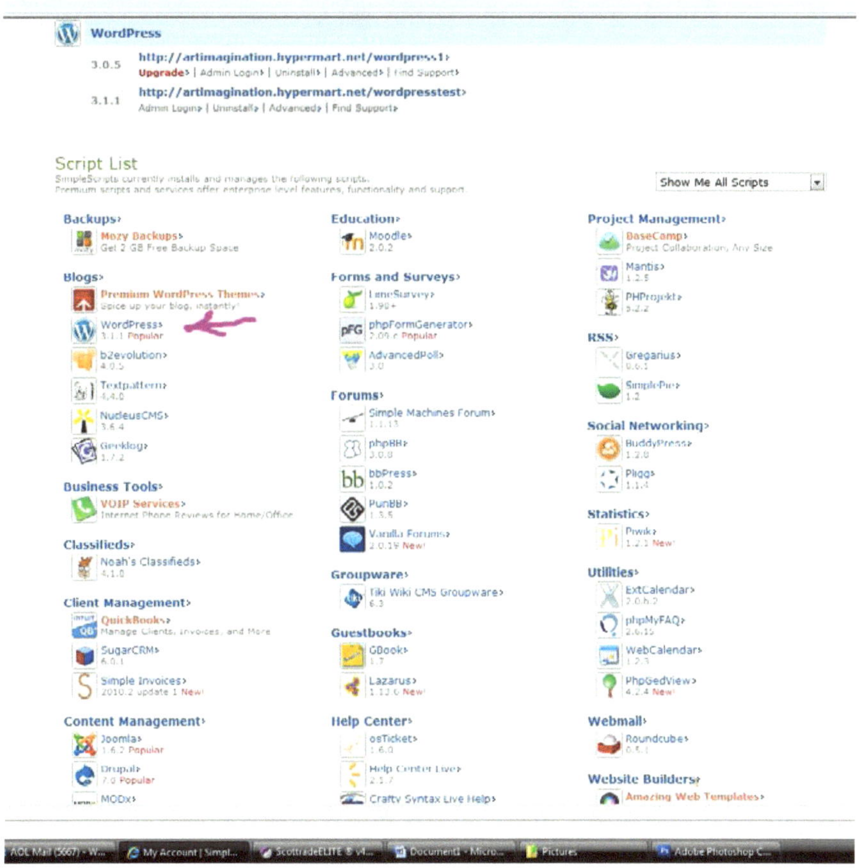

9. *Now click the green "Install" button* — see the pink arrow below:

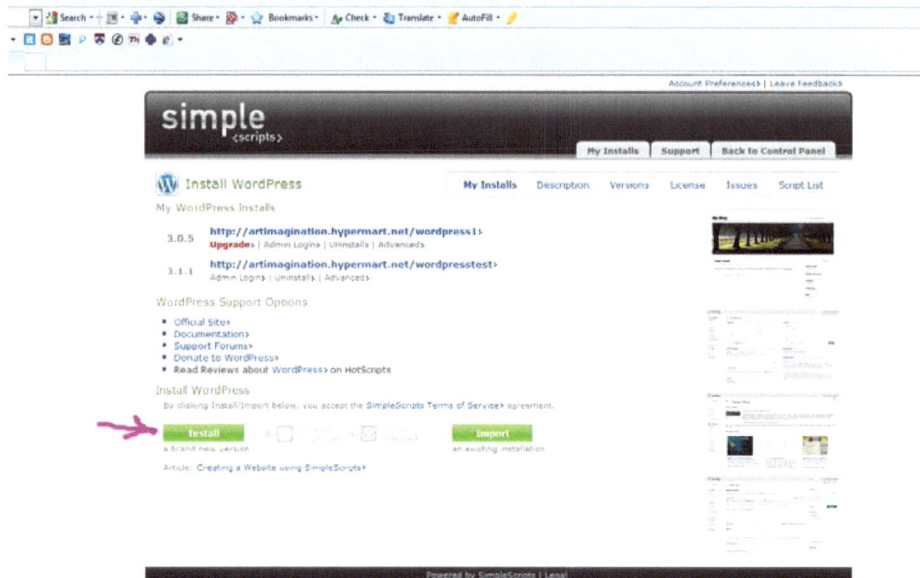

10. *This brings you to the following page, where you get a menu of things to fill in and choose from. Here is the detail, and a picture of the page follows to help you:*

   a. *(a) You need to tell Hypermart which version of the Wordpress software you wish to install. While I have worked with version 3.2, as of the date of this writing for my site I use Wordpress version 3.0.5, which seems very stable to me and seems to work well with many of the free Wordpress add-ons (created by generous outside developers). My personal view is that the older version of Wordpress might be better tested and more stable, and that the add-ons for the older version are well-established and perhaps th9ose add-ons might not yet have evolved or been well-tested to the most recent versions of Wordpress. Therefore, based on my experience, I recommend you either choose version 3.0.5 (the one I primarily use right now) or that you choose a later version of Wordpress that Hypermart lists as the most recent stable version from the*

Hypermart dropdown menu (Hypermart actually indicates which versions are most stable);

b. *(b) On this page you will also type in the name of the directory for your site (like mywordpresstestsite or myshopwordpress or hopethisworks);*

c. *(c) On this page you will also fill in the "advanced options" blanks which enable you to tailor your site. In doing this at a minimum make sure you click "create new database" and click the checkbox in step 3 to indicate you have read the Legal Information and then click complete – see pink arrows below for info for you to fill out. Again, if you use Hypermart you can call them at 877-287-5929 and they can walk you through this.*

11. *After you finish filling in the above information, simply click the green "Complete" button, and the installation starts automatically – in other words, Hypermart installs the free Wordpress software to the directory you chose in step 10(b) above.*

12. *Here is what you will see after you click the "Complete" button, and note that the pink arrow I drew below is where the screen shows you the percent of Wordpress installation in progress, so you can see that it is working:*

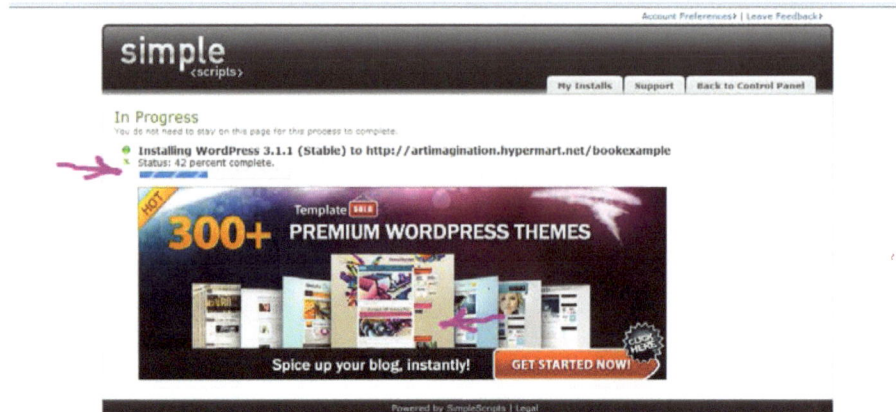

13. *Once installation is complete you will see a window with the information shown below. Which I call the Hypermart Installation Complete confirmation message. Up to this point, you were working inside the Hypermart environment. Now you are ready to work in the Wordpress environment, rather than the Hypermart environment – Congratulations! Your free Wordpress software is installed!* **See my notes in pink below, with some helpful tips:**

```
Installing WordPress 3.1.1 (Stable) to http://artimagination.hypermart.net/bookexample
                                    67
                                  install
Installation Complete! You can access your new website using the following information.
   This information has been e-mailed to artmaestro@aol.com for your convenience.
              Site URL: http://artimagination.hypermart.net/bookexample
           Login URL: http://artimagination.hypermart.net/bookexample/wp-admin
```

Once installation is complete it gives you the above
type message AND sends you an email.
Write down your site URL, login URL and ESPECIALLY YOUR PASSWORD!

What else to learn here:
1. You now have installed the WordPress software onto YOUR own server that you pay for at Hypermart.net (or whomever you choose as host, our example uses Hypermart).
2. Go to the login URL by copying the login URL to your web browser (I tend to use INTERNET EXPLORER).
3. SAVE the Login URL to your favorites on your web browser, so ANYTIME you want to login to change your wordpress site you can go that URL.

Step 3
Logging in to Wordpress

1.   At this point in time, here is what you've done:

-   You've successfully installed the Wordpress software onto your server (either your own server or a free one like http://www.000webhost.comor one that you pay for like http://Hypermart.net

-   As part of the installation process, you will have selected a user name and password. Make sure you save this information!

-   The next step is to actually log in to the Wordpress software now resident on your server and start creating your site using the Wordpress software environment.

2.   How to Login:

-   If you used Hypermart as a host, your Wordpress login URL will have been given to you automatically both by an email sent to you and by an Installation Complete confirmation message like the one shown in Chapter 2, Step 12. Hypermart users can therefore go to their Wordpress login URL by simply copying the login URL from the Hypermart Installation Complete confirmation message into their browser (and bookmarking the address for future use).

-   For all Wordpress users, the login URL always ends in wp-admin. An example of a Wordpress login URL therefore would be something like http://yourwebsitename.com/wp-admin. If you created a subdirectory on your server to store all your Wordpress related work, then your Wordpress login URL would be something like http://yourwebsitename.com/yoursubdirectoryname/wp-admin. If you get confused, remember, the Wordpress login URL is the one that ends in /wp-admin.

-   All of you should make sure you save the login URL and password somewhere.

17

3. *WHAT IS THE DIFFERENCE BETWEEN THE "WORDPRESS LOGIN URL" AND MY WEBSITE URL? The Wordpress login URL is DIFFERENT from your website URL, as follows:*

- *The "Wordpress login URL" is the web address where you go to create and maintain your website. This is where all the behind the scenes work is done on your site. No one but you, the administrator of your website, gets to go to this workspace (unless you invite them and give them the password, which should be kept secret).*

- *Your website URL, on the other hand, is the public web address you advertise on your business card. Your website URL is the address for your finished website. Anyone can go here to see your website. Your website URL is what would show up on Google search, for example.*

- *If you get confused, remember, the Wordpress login URL is the one that ends in /wp-admin while the website URL is generally the one that ends in .com or .net*

4. *NOW TO LOG IN TO CREATE YOUR WEBSUITE: When you type your Wordpress login URL (the URL that ends in /wp-admin) into your internet browser, you will see a screen that looks like this:*

- *Note: This login web page is actually running off of your server, not the wordpress.org server!*

Instructions on how to login:

- *As part of the installation process, you will have selected a user name and password. Simply type in your user name and password in the blanks on the Wordpress login screen, like the login screen shown above.*

- *Press the blue "Log In" button*

- *This will take you to the Wordpress software design environment, known as the "Dashboard," where you can create your website, the subject of the next chapter. Congratulations!*

Part 2 – Working in Wordpress
Quick Steps to Creating Your Basic Wordpress Site

The "Theme" (under the Appearance" menu in the Wordpress "Dashboard") is T wenty Ten 1.1, but I changed the header.

Custom "header" image created using Adobe Photoshop. Image size for header is 940 pixels wide by 198 pixels tall.

Simple First Page, with Wordpress text still in it

"Search" widget

"Text" widget

"Meta" widget

*Step 4 – **CHOOSING THE THEME OR TEMPLATE TO USE AS THE BASE STRUCTURE OF YOUR SITE***

1. *Now that you have successfully logged into Wordpress, you will see the following screen (what you see may very SLIGHTLY depending on the specific version of Wordpress you chose to use, but the overall logic and structure is the same, so don't panic!) – You are now ready to start building your first Wordpress site!*

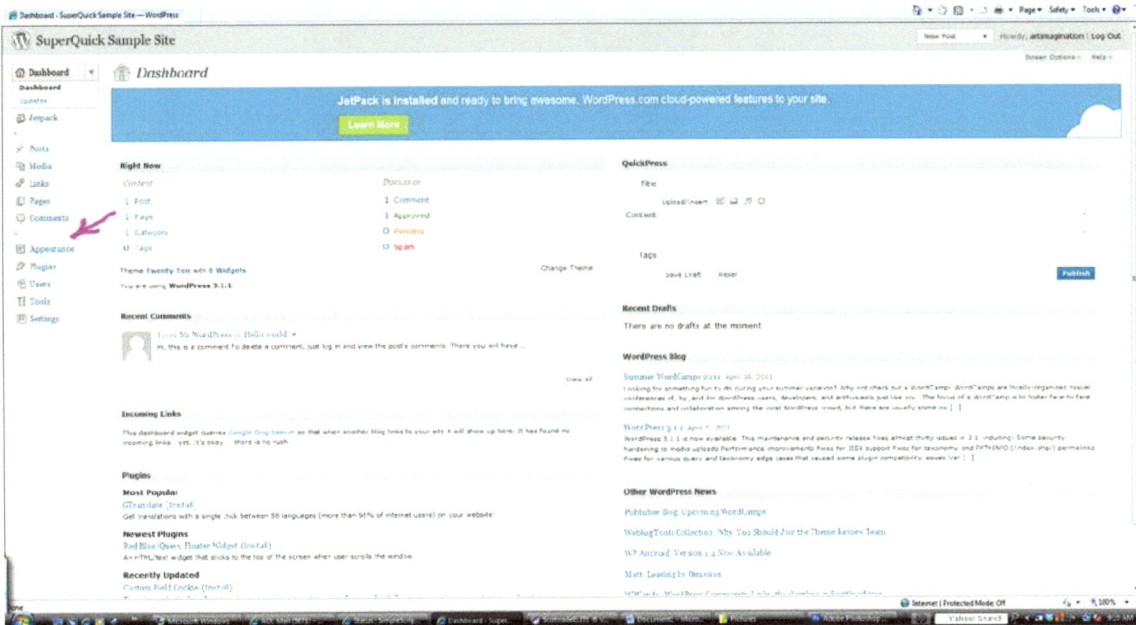

2. *The first step is to click the "Appearance" menu (see the pink arrow I drew in the picture above), which then gives you a drop-down menu (shown in 3 next).*

3. Choose "Themes" from this drop-down menu – see where the pink arrow is below.

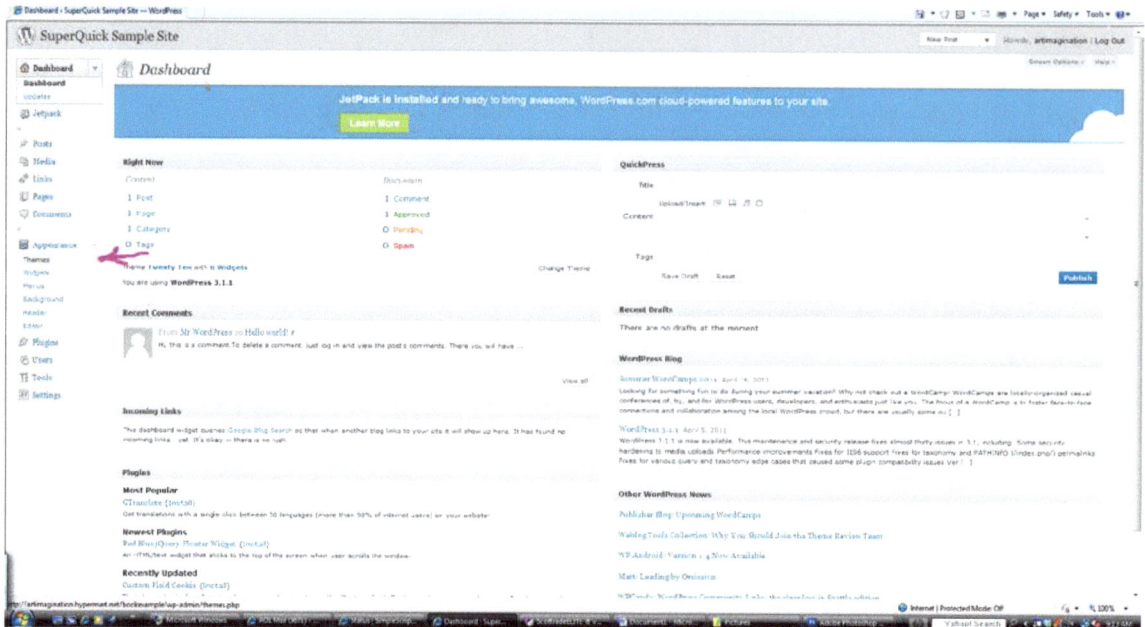

4. "Themes" is where you get to pick the template that will be the base design of your site. This therefore is an important choice, but luckily, the default theme is quite good, and the one I use.

5. When you browse the themes, several things can be important factors – where you can place "widgets", how many menus you can have, how many columns of text it will have, etc. While you can always change your "Theme" later, there is risk that you might lose some of your hard work when you do, so it is better to start with a basic structure you like.

6. I really like the default "Theme" called Twenty Ten, which has "widgets" on the right side and also at the bottom of each web page you create, and I think overall this Twenty Ten Theme provides a clean look, with a customizable menu at top that can support multiple tabs.

7. In general, when you look at "Themes" look more at the underlying structure of the site such as where the columns are - don't be swayed by the photos on the site samples, unless you plan on using Wordpress photos instead of your own. Remember that you can actually change the images on the site, and this book shows you how. If you aren't sure, go with the default theme Twenty Ten.

8. More specifically, as shown below, the default theme is called "Twenty Ten" – that's the one I use, and it works fine.

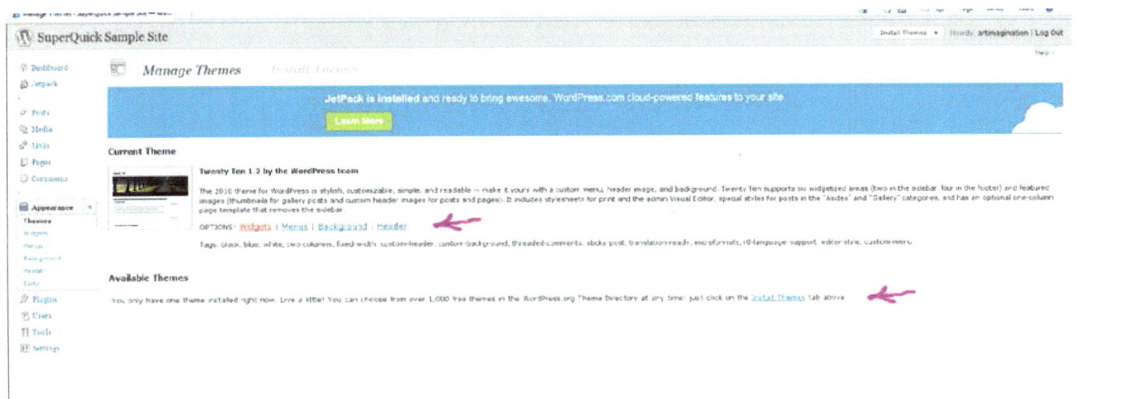

9. Summary:

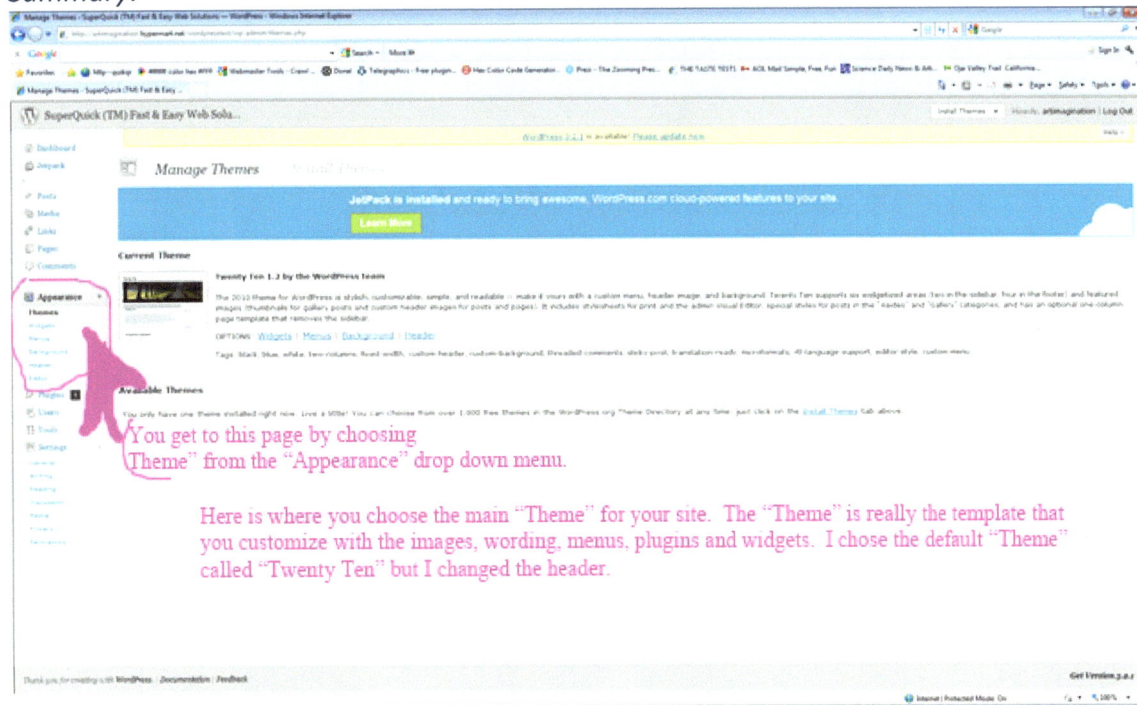

You get to this page by choosing
Theme" from the "Appearance" drop down menu.

Here is where you choose the main "Theme" for your site. The "Theme" is really the template that you customize with the images, wording, menus, plugins and widgets. I chose the default "Theme" called "Twenty Ten" but I changed the header.

You have now chosen the "theme" or template that will be the main structure or bones of your site. Now it is time to dress up whatever "Theme" you chose with your text and images. In other words, it is time to customize your "Theme" to make it your own!

I start customizing my theme first by adding my own graphic to the header – **see Step 5 which shows you how to customize the header with your own graphic**!

Step 5 - CUSTOMIZING THE "HEADER" IMAGE FOR YOUR SITE:

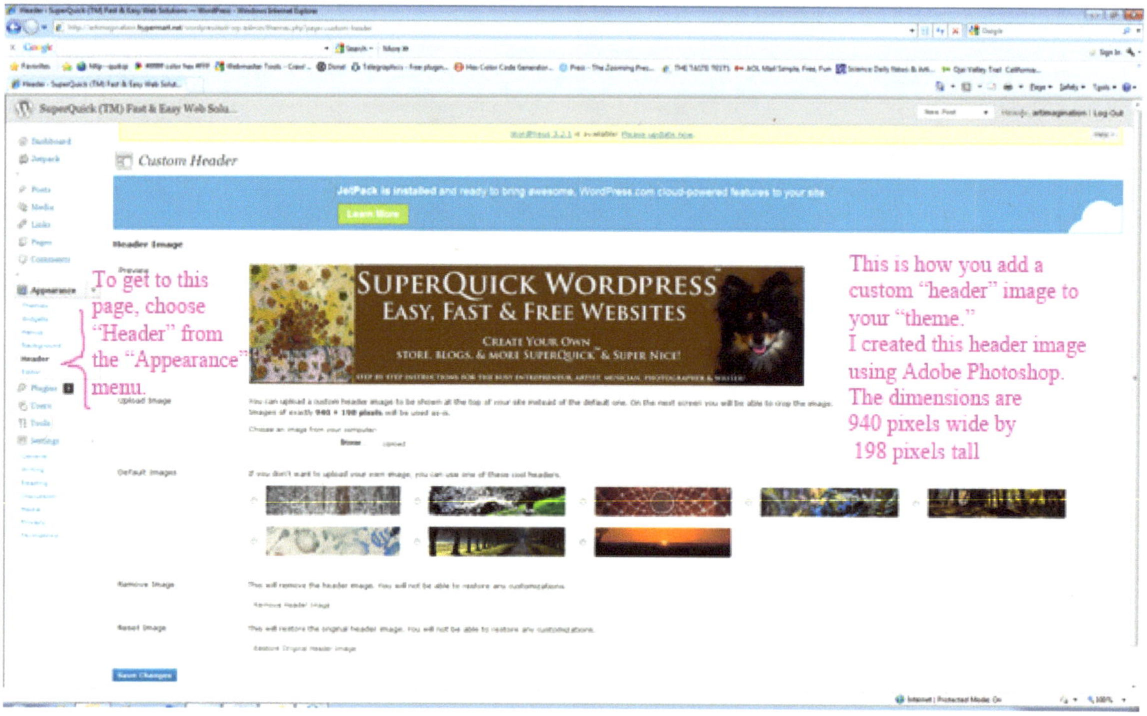

1. Choose "Header" from the Dashboard "Appearance" dropdown menu, as shown above.

Note: You can also get to the header customization page, as shown below, by choosing "Header" while on the "Manage Themes" page – whichever is easiest for you:

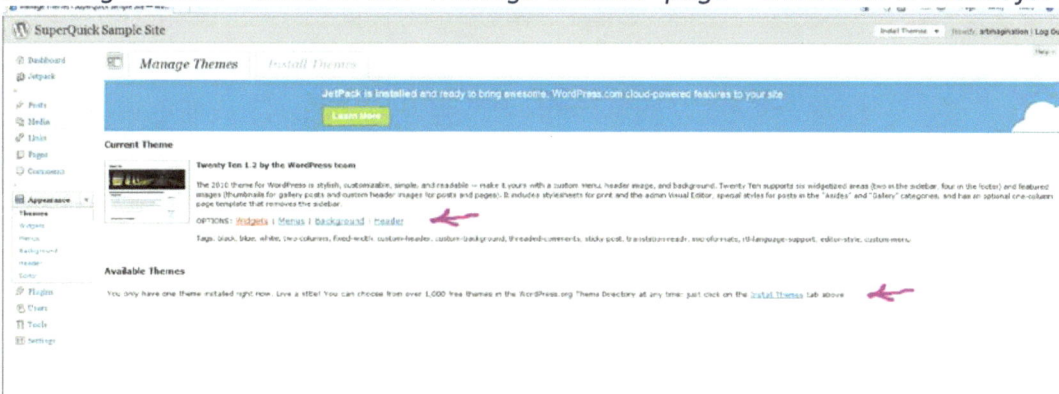

2. By clicking "Header" as shown in the preceding step, you will then see the following screen, where you can browse images stored on your own computer to upload to your site and use as the header image for your site. That's pretty easy! No "ftp" required to do that – the free Wordpress software does that for you! Hurray! See the pink arrow below to see where the "browse" button is.

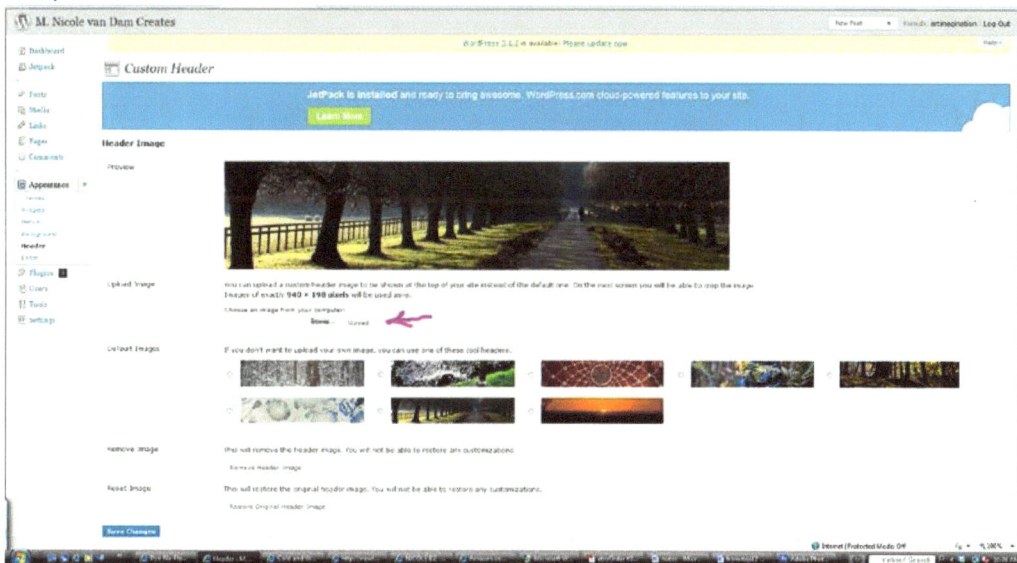

NOTE: To customize your site, of course you need to have a few images already stored on your computer with which to customize! How to create a header image: In the example below I created, using Adobe Photoshop, an image that was 940 pixels wide and 198 pixels tall. See Appendix for illustrated detail on how to size an image using Adobe Photoshop. Adobe Photoshop is indispensable software if you want to do

customized things on the web! (I am not paid by Adobe to say that!)

3. *Following is the header image I created for this book example using Adobe Photoshop. The image is a jpeg* 940 pixels wide and 198 pixels tall. *To create this wide but short image, I used Photoshop to combine 2 pre-existing square-shaped images (one image had flowers, one image is of a dog, and using Photoshop I placed an image at each end of this wide rectangle for balance). In the wide space between the two images, I used Photoshop to easily insert text, and I chose a colored background designed to tie it all together (using Photoshop's color matching eyedropper tool to match color to the dog image's pre-existing background). It all works together to make one wide, short image of the size needed for Wordpress. While in Photoshop I saved this image to my computer hard drive as "SampleSiteBanner.jpg".*

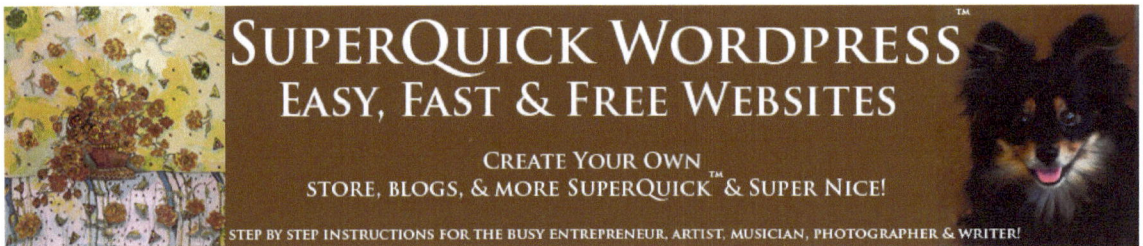

4. *In our example I then used Wordpress (See pink arrow below) to browse to the SampleSiteBanner.jpg image that was stored on my computer – again this is the image that I had previously created with Adobe Photoshop:*

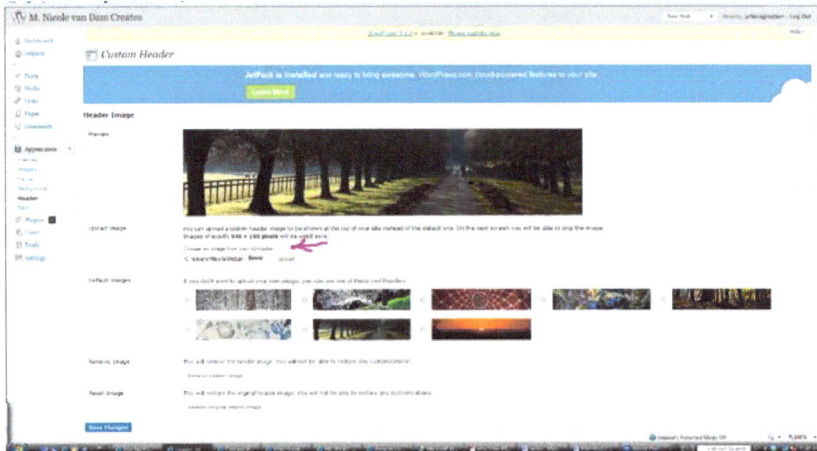

Taking the above step generated the following result:

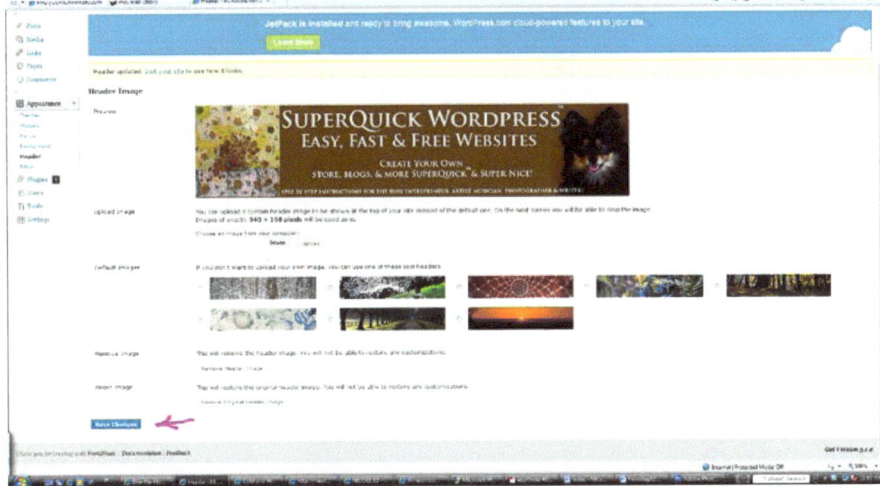

I like the result so I then click the blue "Save Changes" button (see pink arrow above)

Behind the Scenes Tidbit: What also resulted is that the design that I had saved on my computer was uploaded via the Wordpress software to my server on the web! This is important for you know the difference: The image on my computer was NOT uploaded to Wordpress.org; rather the image was automatically uploaded to the Hypermart server that I rent on the web! In other words, if you rent a server at ABC Corp, then your image would be uploaded from your computer to your server at ABC Corp. Wordpress.org does not house your images for you.   This uploading of your images to YOUR server is a good thing, because it gives you slightly more control over your images and who has access to them, including ease of removing the images in the future should you so choose.

Step 6 - CHOOSING AND CUSTOMIZING THE "WIDGETS" USED ON YOUR SITE

The next step to customizing your Wordpress site is to choose and customize the "widgets" that you want to use on your site. You will like widgets!!! They add functionality and interest to your site, as you will see on the following pages.

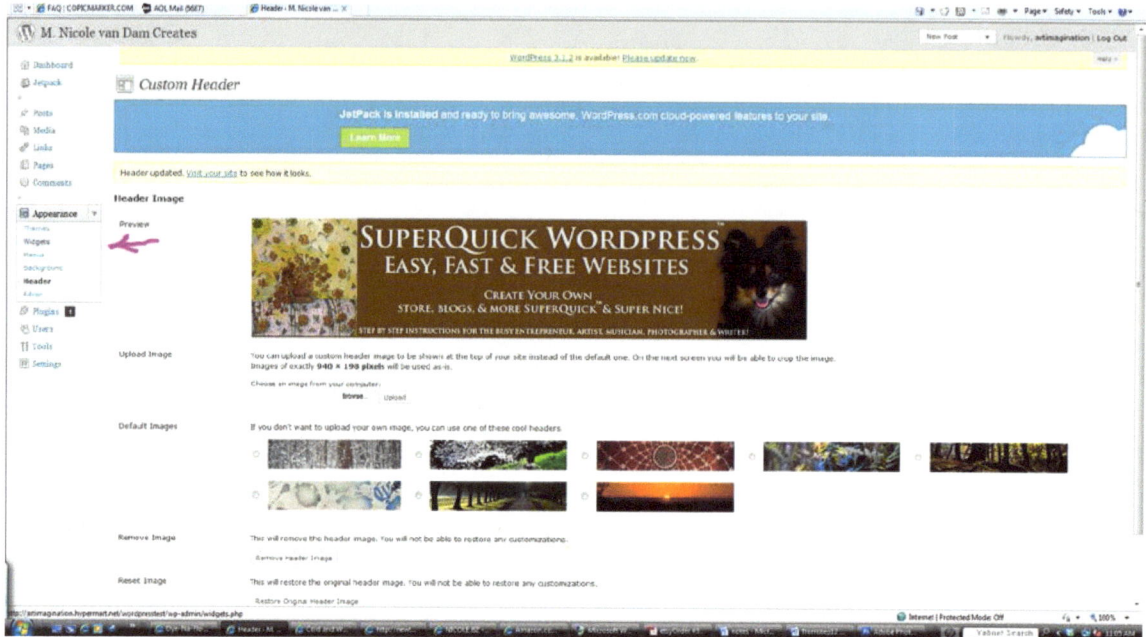

1. The first step in mastering "widgets" is finding where the workspace is for them! As shown in the image above with the pink arrow, to find "Widgets" you go to the "Appearance" drop-down menu, and then you click on "Widgets." This will bring you to the following page.

2. *The "Widgets" Workspace:*

   ILLUSTRATION WIDGET-1 below shows the Widgets workspace, which is divided into several areas, which I have color-coded for you:

   a. **The area circled in green are the available widgets that automatically come standard with Wordpress.** _You can add more, for free_. *For now, let's start with these pre-existing widgets, as there is a lot you can do with them. You will see that there is a pre-existing widget to easily set up a calendar of your events to display on your website, as well as widget that will allow you to easily add a "search" feature to your site that enables users to search your site. There is also a widget that lets you easily add a bullet point list links to other webpages. There is also a widget there that will display an archive of your blog posts, and a very useful widget called "meta" that will let you and others log in and subscribe to your site. There is a RSS widget that will allow others to get a feed of the news items on your site, and much more. These widgets that you see here are available widgets that you already have to use.* **GREEN AREA SUMMARY: Here is where you can choose which widgets to add to your site; you add a widget by dragging the widget you choose from the "Available Widgets" shown below to the "Widget Areas" at right sidebar.**

   b. *As stated above, to use one of these available widgets in the green-circled area, you simply drag that widget using your mouse to any of the "widget areas" on the right side of the screen (see the pink line I drew, everything on that right side). If you look at the right column of the screen, you will see things called "Primary Widget Area" and a "Secondary Widget Area" as well as a First, Second, Third and Fourth Footer Widget Areas.* **PINK AREA AS SHOWN IN THIS SCREEN CAPTURE:** *When you first go to the widgets page, IF you chose "Twenty Ten "as your "theme" in Step 4 of this* book, then you will automatically find some widgets have already been placed for you in the "Primary Widget Area (designated by the pink highlighted area in my drawing above). These widgets that are already there in the "Primary Widget Area" are the "widgets" that the Twenty Ten theme we chose in Step 4 automatically inserts for you as defaults. If you choose a different theme than Twenty Ten in Step 4 to start with, then your default widgets showing in the Primary Widget Area might be different.

ILLUSTRATION WIDGET-1 Repeated for ease of reference

• *You can ALWAYS at any time, now or later, eliminate whichever widgets you don't like by dragging them to the **"Inactive Widgets" BLUE area** in the illustration above.*

• *You can ALWAYS at any time, now or later, add more widgets simply by dragging them with your mouse from the selection of widgets shown in the "Available Widgets" area above to the widgets areas sidebar at right.*

• *You can ALWAYS at any time, now or later, move widgets to any widget area you see notated at the right sidebar. Note that with this "Twenty Ten" theme that we chose in Step 4, you can have widgets to the right of the site and below the site. Other themes might give you different widget areas.*

30

ILLUSTRATION WIDGET-1 Repeated for ease of reference

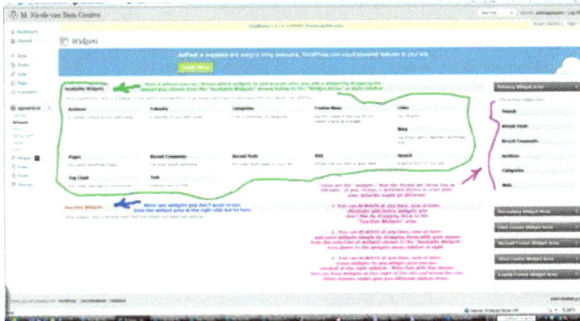

c. The "Primary Widget Area"(to the right of the pink line above) is what will ultimately show up in the upper right side of your website; while the "Secondary Widget Area" will be what shows up just below that, still on the right side, but just below the Primary Widget Area. The four "Footer" widget areas represent four columns of footers that line up on the bottom of your website, the "First Footer Widget Area" corresponding to the furthest left column at the bottom of your website, through the "Fourth Footer Widget Area" being the furthest right footer column, again at the bottom of your website.

d. YOU DON'T NEED TO USE ALL THE AVAILABLE WIDGETS

e. YOU DON'T NEED TO USE ALL THE WIDGET AREAS.

f. The available widgets and the various widget areas are just OPTIONS available to this particular "Theme" we chose called "Twenty Ten."

g. If you chose in Step 4 a different "theme" than "Twenty Ten," your widget areas might be different. For example, there are no widgets areas that will appear on the left side of a website based on the "Twenty Ten" theme – instead widgets are only available on the right side and bottom. If you want widgets on the left side instead of the right side, you need to choose a different theme than Twenty Ten. This is one of the reasons why choosing the right theme from the start is important.

3. **CHANGING THE WIDGETS YOU USE:**
   ILLUSTRATION WIDGET-1 (repeated for ease of reference):

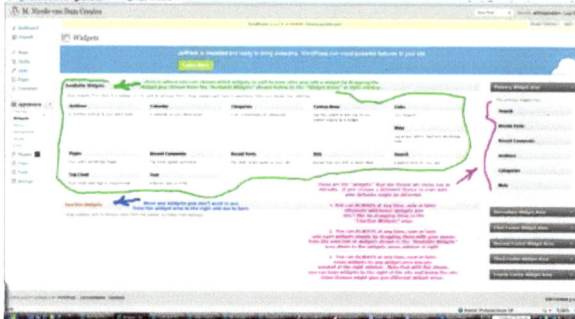

The "Primary Widget Area" is to the right of the pink line in ILLUSTRATION *WIDGET-1 above.* **Enlarged, below, the "Primary Widget Area' for "Twenty Ten" theme looks like this:**

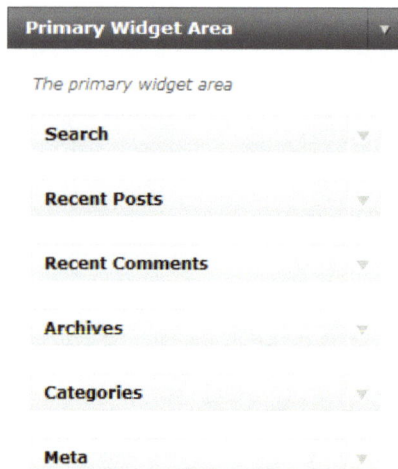

Again, as stated in subsection "b" above, when you look at the widgets screen, you will see that some widgets by default, just to get you started, are already in use in the "Primary Widget Area" – As shown above, in the "Primary Widget Area" you will see the "Search" widget in use, for example, as well as "Recent Posts," "Recent Comments," "Archives," "Categories" and "Meta" widgets. **You don't need to keep these widgets there**! *You can drag any one (or more) of these widgets away from the "Primary Widget Area" to the area called "Inactive Widgets" (see the blue arrow*

in ILLUSTRATION WIDGET-1 above for where the "Inactive Widgets" area begins). If you change your mind, you can always drag the widgets back into use again simply by putting them back into one of the active widget areas on the right column of the screen. A DETAILED EXAMPLE OF CUSTOMIZING YOUR WIDGETS CHOICES (SEE ILLUSTRATION WIDGETS-2) FOLLOWS ON THE NEXT PAGES.

4. *You can also reorder widgets that you are using, by simply dragging and dropping them to where you want them to be in the widget area hierarchy.*
5. *You can also drag and drop any widget among ANY widget areas (you can move something from a primary widget area to the "Third Footer widget area", for example).*
6. *You can also use the same widget multiple times, in different widget areas or in the same widget area. For example, you might wish to use the "Search" widget more than once, such as once in the "Primary Widget Area" and once in the "Fourth Footer Widget Area."*
7. *In other words, getting all the functionality of search or a calendar or any other widget is as easy as dragging and dropping the widget from the available widgets area to the widget area that you want it to appear – such as dragging the "Calendar" widget from the "Available Widget Area" to the "Primary Widget Area."*
8. *These widgets that you choose will then appear in the same place on every page of your site.*

ILLUSTRATION WIDGET-2 below shows customizing your widgets:

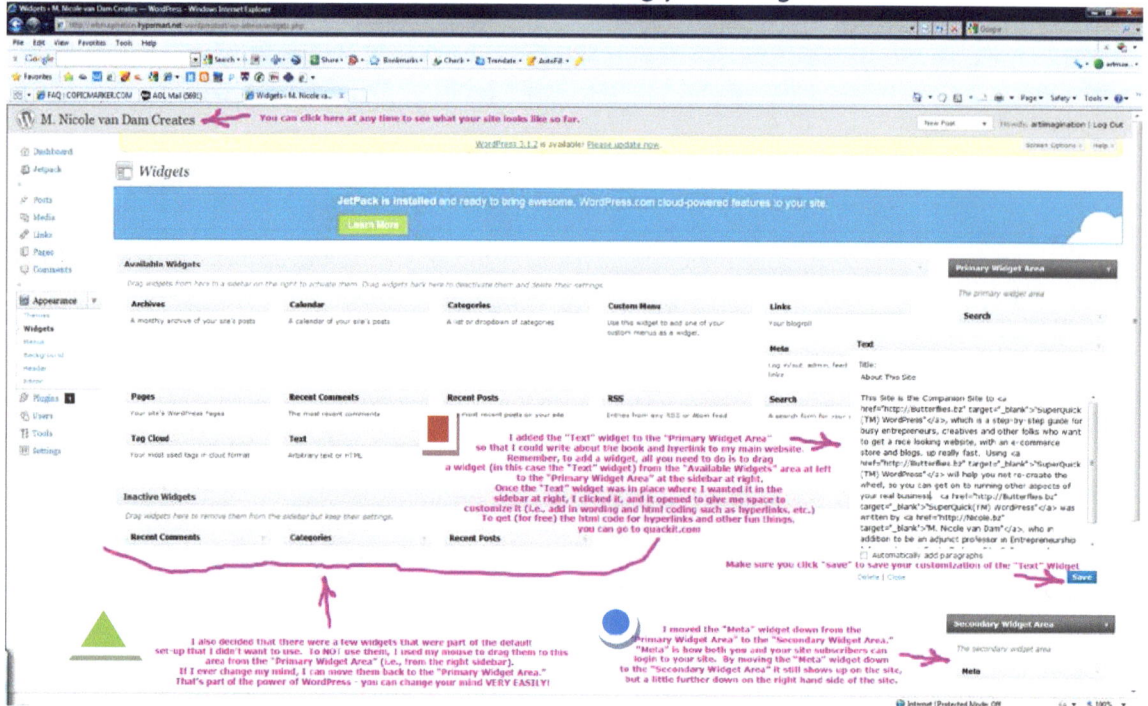

What the pink text says above:

■ *I added the "Text" widget to the "Primary Widget Area "so that I could write about the book and hyperlink to my main website. Remember, to add a widget, all you need to do is to drag a widget (in this case the "Text" widget) from the "Available Widgets" area at left to the "Primary Widget Area" at the sidebar at right. Once the "Text" widget was in place where I wanted it in the sidebar at right, I clicked it, and it opened to give me space to customize it (i.e., add in wording and html coding such as hyperlinks, etc.) To get (for free) the html code for hyperlinks and other fun things, you can go to quackit.com   Make sure you click "Save" to save your customization of the "Text" widget.*

● *I moved the "Meta" widget down from the "Primary Widget Area" to the "Secondary Widget Area." "Meta" is how both you and your site subscribers can login to your site. By moving the "Meta" widget down to the "Secondary Widget Area" it still shows up on the site, but a little further down on the right hand side of the site.*

▲ *I also decided that there were a few widgets that were part of the default set-up that I didn't want to use. To NOT use them, I used my mouse to drag them to this area from the "Primary Widget Area" (i.e., from the right sidebar). If I ever change my mind, I can move them back to the "Primary Widget Area."*

34

That's part of the power of Wordpress - you can change your mind VERY EASILY!

9. *Summary: In the example above, I decided NOT to use any of the "Recent Posts," "Recent Comments," "Archives" or "Categories" widgets, so I dragged them from the "Primary Widget Area" to the "Inactive Widgets" area.*
10. *That left the "Search" widget and the "Meta" widget in the Primary Widget Area.*
11. *I then decided to add a "Text" widget by dragging it to the "Primary Widget Area" from the "Available Widget" area.*
12. *Once I dragged the "Text" widget from the "Available Widgets" area to the "Primary Widget Area" then I had to customize the "Text" widget.*
13. *To customize a widget: You customize a particular widget by clicking on that particular widget's name (in this case "Text") as it sits in the widget area in which you placed it (in this case, as it sits in the "Primary Widget Area"). Below is an example of how I customized the Text widget in the Primary Widget area – by clicking on the widget name "Text" the widget box expands as shown below.*

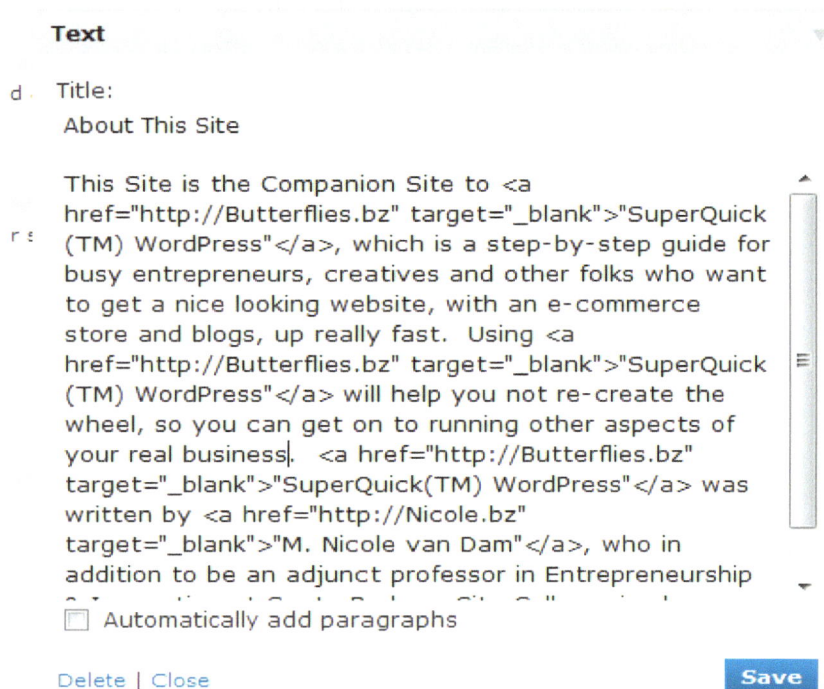

Text   ▼

d   Title:

    About This Site

r   This Site is the Companion Site to <a href="http://Butterflies.bz" target="_blank">"SuperQuick (TM) WordPress"</a>, which is a step-by-step guide for busy entrepreneurs, creatives and other folks who want to get a nice looking website, with an e-commerce store and blogs, up really fast. Using <a href="http://Butterflies.bz" target="_blank">"SuperQuick (TM) WordPress"</a> will help you not re-create the wheel, so you can get on to running other aspects of your real business. <a href="http://Butterflies.bz" target="_blank">"SuperQuick(TM) WordPress"</a> was written by <a href="http://Nicole.bz" target="_blank">"M. Nicole van Dam"</a>, who in addition to be an adjunct professor in Entrepreneurship

☐ Automatically add paragraphs

Delete | Close   **Save**

Now I can enter any text (including html for things such as links and photos) into the text box. When I am done customizing, I click the blue "Save" button that is in that text box.

35

14. *Once I am done, I want to preview my work. I preview my work by clicking the name of my site in the upper right corner of the screen - see the red arrow below. In this example the name of my site is "M. Nicole van Dam Creates" — see illustration below:*

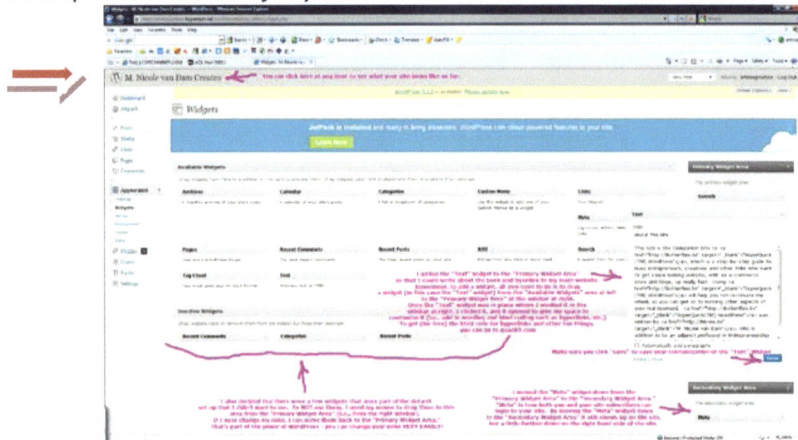

Clicking the name of my site (by the red arrow above) shows me the results of the changes I have made to the widgets. Here is the result of my work:

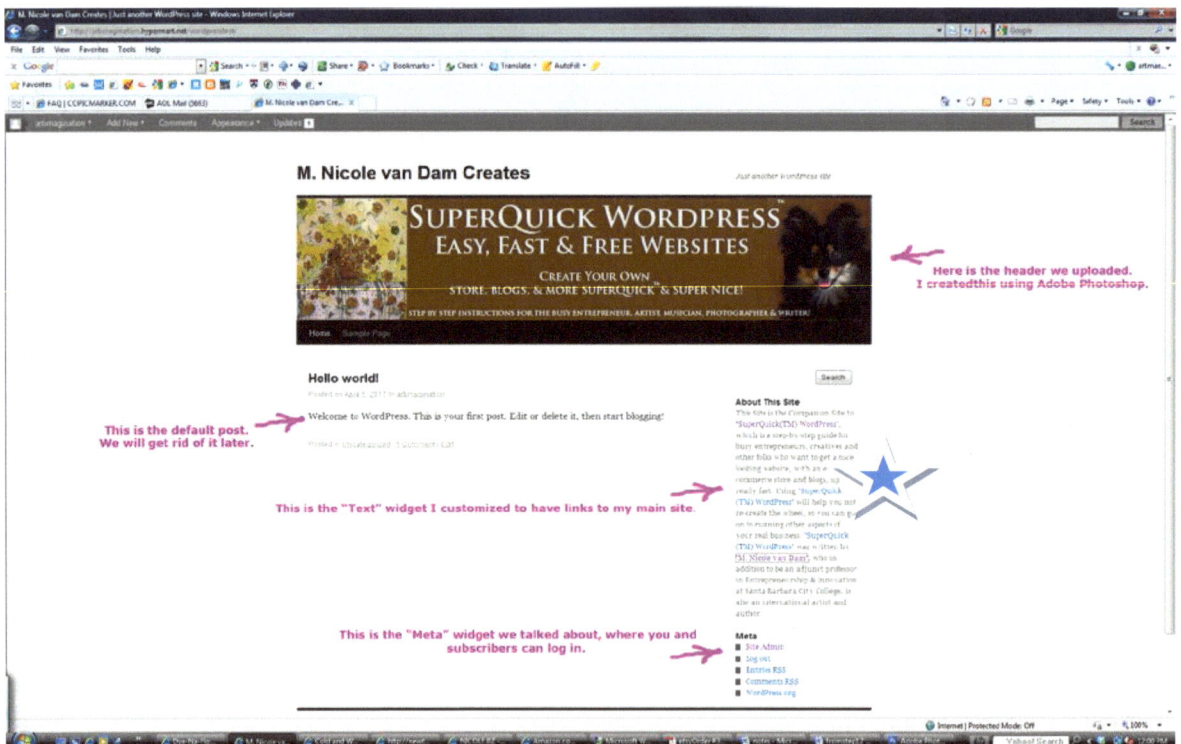

The ⭐ *was inserted into this illustration to help you find the "Text" widget.*

PICTORAL SUMMARY OF THE WIDGETS PAGE:

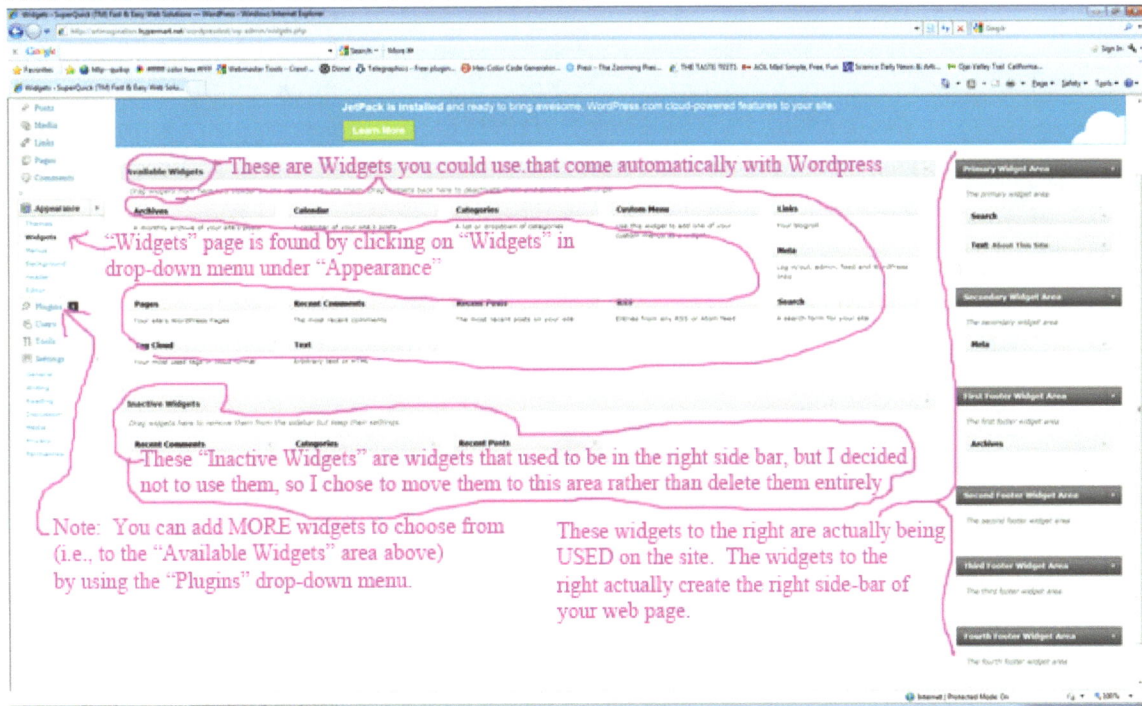

The annotations on the screenshot read:

These are Widgets you could use.that come automatically with Wordpress

"Widgets" page is found by clicking on "Widgets" in drop-down menu under "Appearance"

These "Inactive Widgets" are widgets that used to be in the right side bar, but I decided not to use them, so I chose to move them to this area rather than delete them entirely

Note: You can add MORE widgets to choose from (i.e., to the "Available Widgets" area above) by using the "Plugins" drop-down menu.

These widgets to the right are actually being USED on the site. The widgets to the right actually create the right side-bar of your web page.

15. *In the earlier versions of Wordpress you can hit the back arrow on your browser to return from reviewing the results of your work to where you were (i.e., to return to the widgets workspace), while in later versions of Wordpress (shown below is version 3.1.2) you can also click the "Appearance" menu choice at the top of the screen and then choose "Widgets" from the "Appearance" drop down menu to return to the widgets workspace page.*

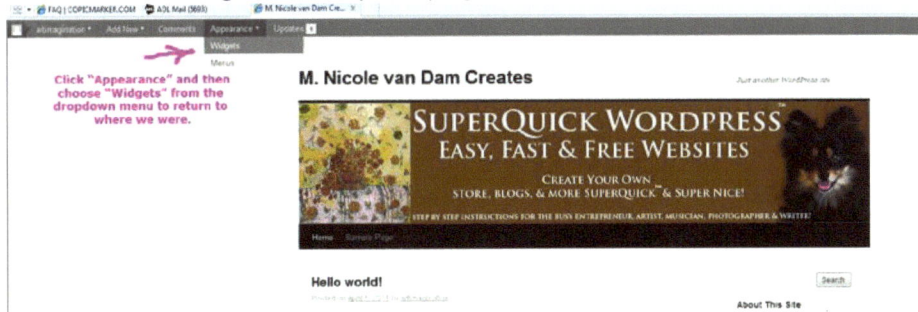

Click "Appearance" and then choose "Widgets" from the dropdown menu to return to where we were.

We will go over more fun and useful widgets in Part 5 - Advanced Design, Plugins and Widgets

Step 7 - CUSTOMIZING THE "SETTINGS" FOR YOUR SITE, SUCH AS SITE TITLE, AND SETTING PREFERENCES FOR USER COMMENTS

Now that we've returned to the Widget workspace, it's time to move on to customizing other parts of the site, such as the site title. You do this by clicking on the "Settings" menu choice, shown by the pink arrow below:

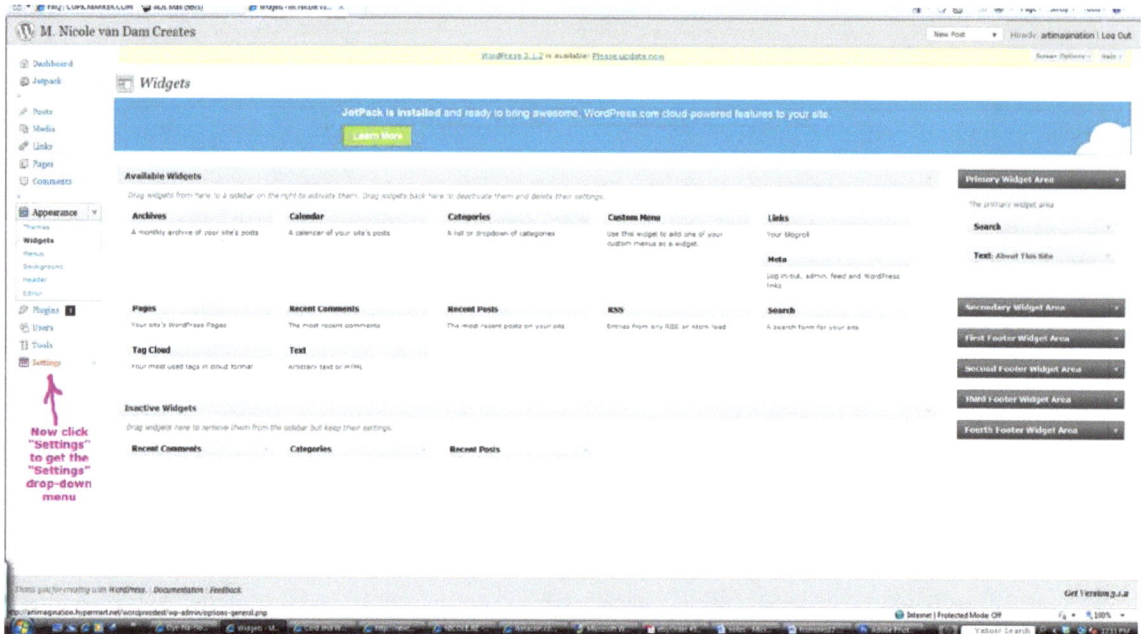

1. *Once you click on "Settings" as shown above, you can customize many things, including Site Title and Tagline and email address – let's do those three things now. In the example I put the Site title as "SuperQuick ™ Fast & Easy Web Solutions" and I put the tagline as "Fast & Easy Web Solutions by M. Nicole van Dam." I also put in a default email address for the website to use for me. Once you do those three things for your site, remember to click the blue save box, all as shown by the pink arrows*

38

below.

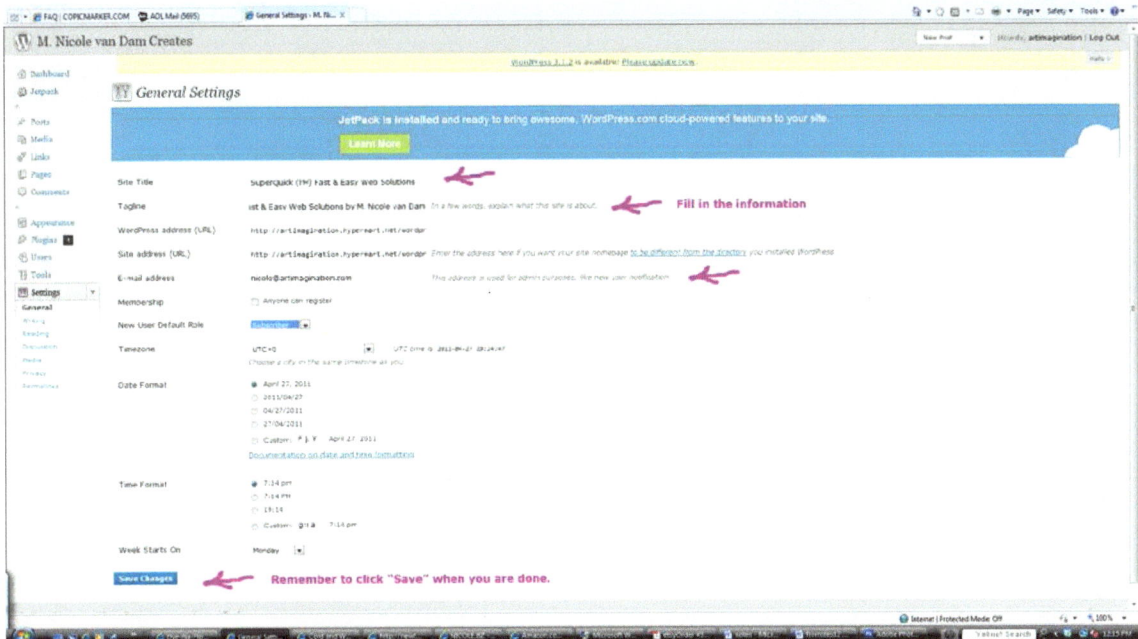

2. *Another thing you will see- the Settings menu on the left Dashboard menu bar has its own Settings drop down menu –see the enlargement below:*

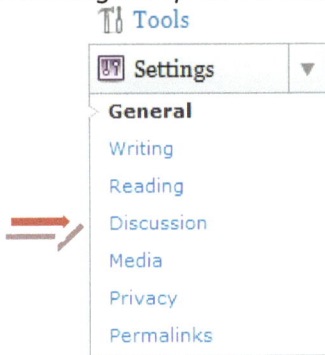

For the next step please click the" Discussion" choice on the Settings drop down menu (see the red arrow above) and set your permissions. "Discussions" is where you pick settings to help prevent spam bloggers, etc.

3. Here below are the settings I chose for the "Discussion" tab. I like to pre-approve posts and require posters register/subscribe to my site before they can post anything (hence the usefulness of the "Meta" widget). **Make sure, when you are through, that you click the save changes box at the bottom left of the discussions page to save your choices.   You can always change things later.**

4. *Following is the result of our work so far!*

  🟢 *You can see the "SuperQuick ™ Fast & Easy Web Solutions" language is now the "title" of the site.*

  🔻 *You can also see the" tagline" just to the right of the title, in much smaller print, is now also what we chose ("Fast & Easy Web Solutions by M. Nicole van Dam").*

  ⬅ *You can see also the header we customized in an earlier chapter, and*

  ⬅ *You can see the widgets we chose, in the right column.*

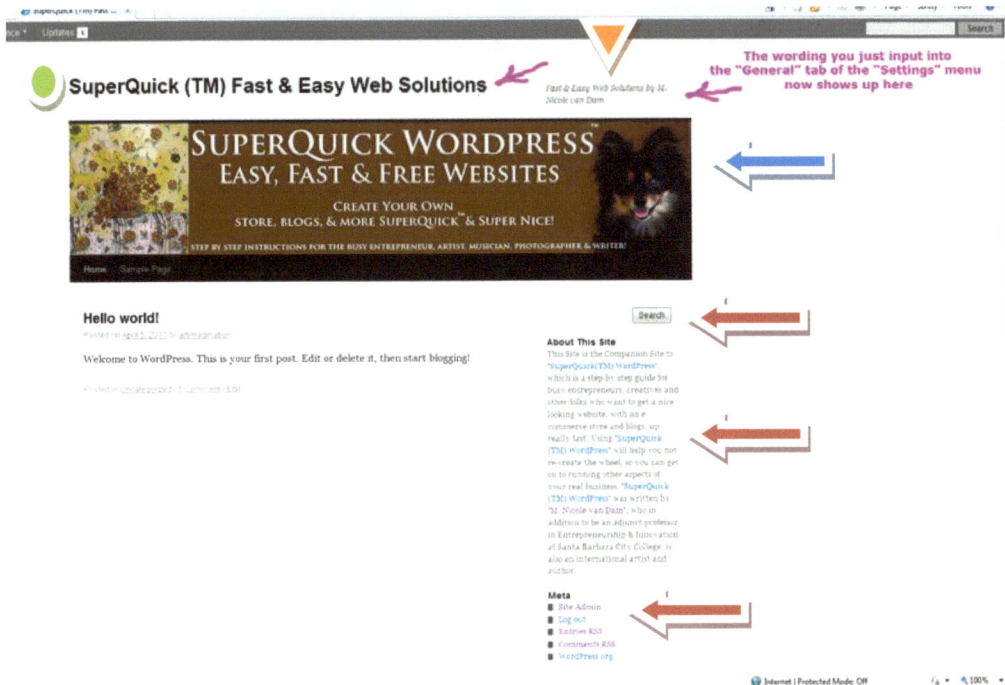

5. *To Return to the Wordpress "Dashboard" for the next step:*
   In the earlier versions of Wordpress you can hit the back arrow on your browser to return from reviewing the results of your work to where you were, while in later versions of Wordpress (shown below is version 3.1.2) you can also click your user name at the top of the screen and then a drop down menu will appear, as shown below - choose "Dashboard" from that drop down menu to return to the Dashboard to go to the next step.

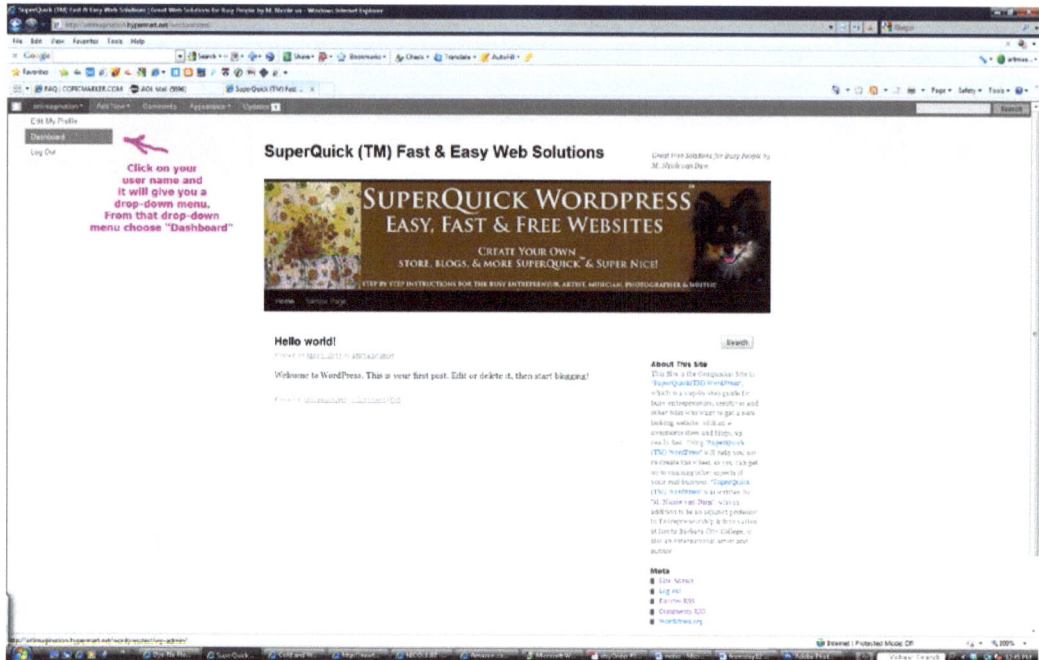

Step 8 – Installing "Jetpack" Capabilities

1. *I see this as an "optional step" – in other words, I personally don't think Jetpack is necessary, but it gives you some interesting tools and is available easily in later versions (3.1.2 and later) of Wordpress.* Here is how you set up "Jetpack" if you choose to:

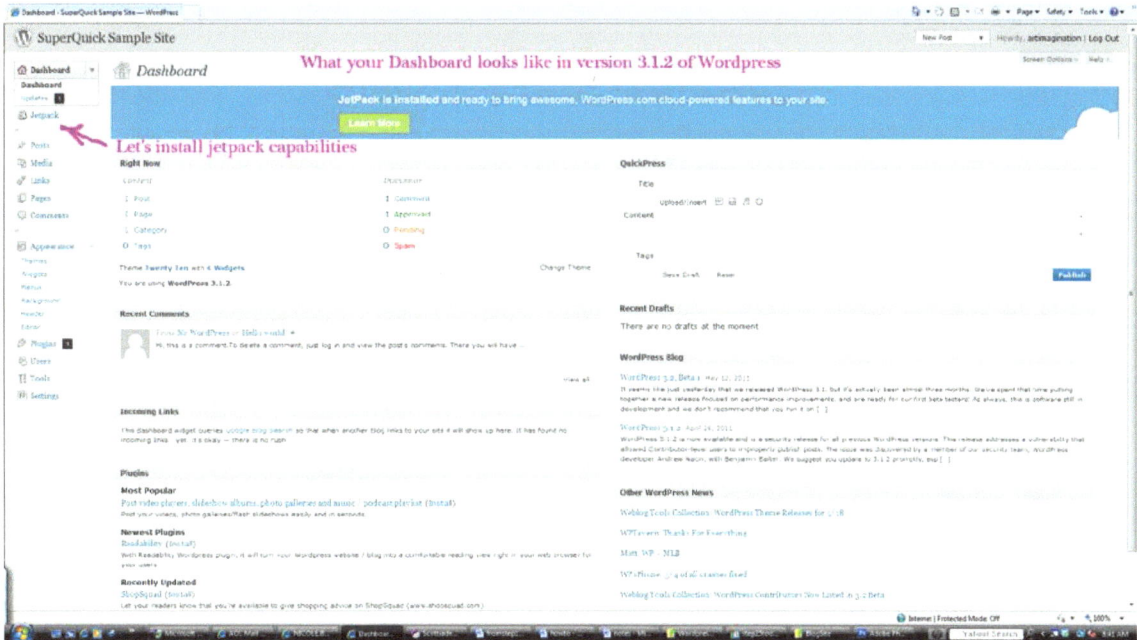

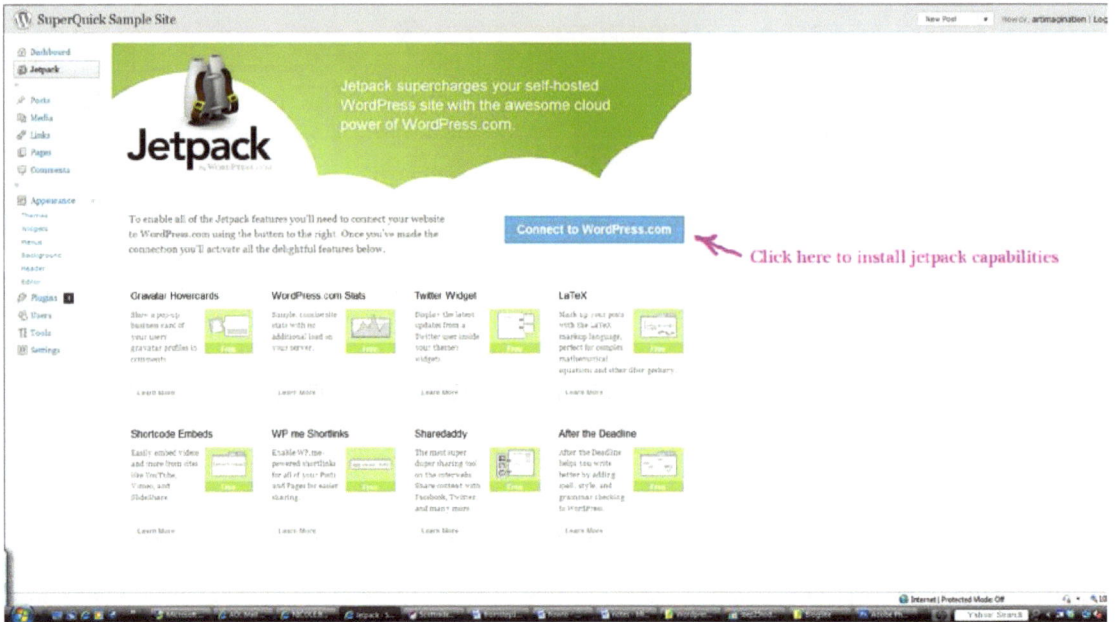

Click here to install jetpack capabilities

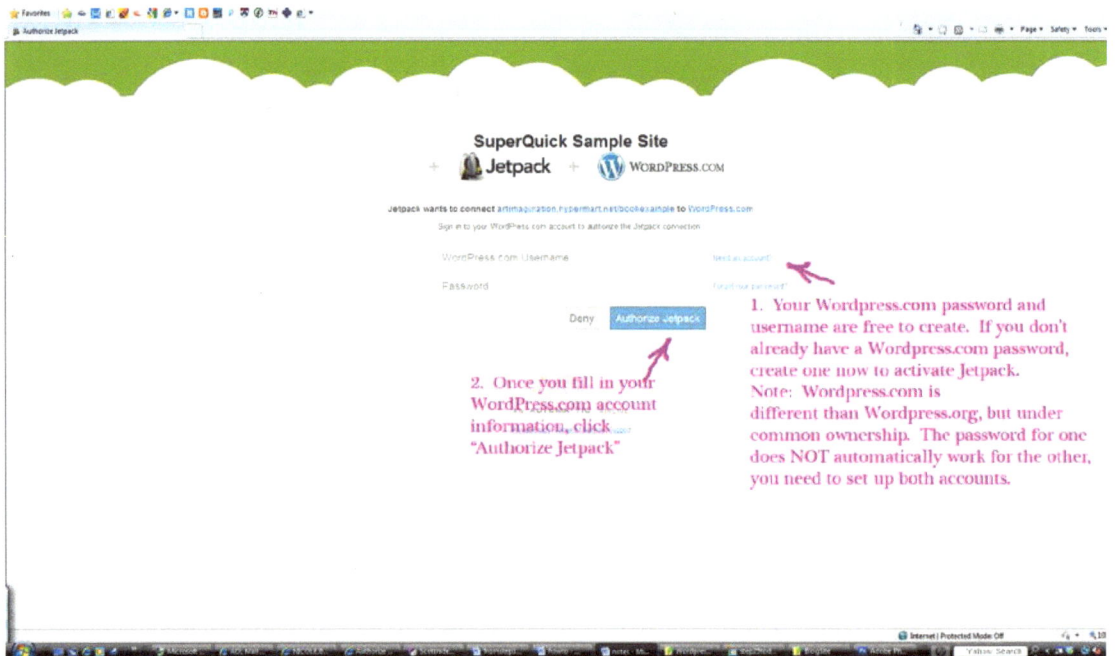

1. Your Wordpress.com password and username are free to create. If you don't already have a Wordpress.com password, create one now to activate Jetpack. Note: Wordpress.com is different than Wordpress.org, but under common ownership. The password for one does NOT automatically work for the other, you need to set up both accounts.

2. Once you fill in your WordPress.com account information, click "Authorize Jetpack"

1. Clicking Authorize Jetpack on the previous screen brings you back to your Wordpress.Org dashboard. Now you see all the goodies Jetpack provides you.

3. Some of these Jetpack features need to be configured. To do this, simply click the "Configure" button for that feature. Let's configure this spell checking feature now, by clicking "Configure."

2. You can click "Learn More" to learn more about each feature. This one spell checks your posts, that's handy!

Step 9 – Setting up other Important Wordpress "Dashboard" Preferences

1. Click on "Users" on the Dashboard menu, as shown enlarged (by the red arrow) below:

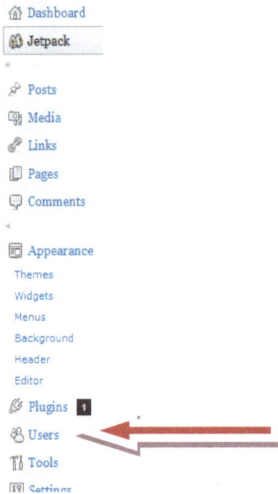

When you click on "Users" you will get a dropdown menu for "Users" as shown below:

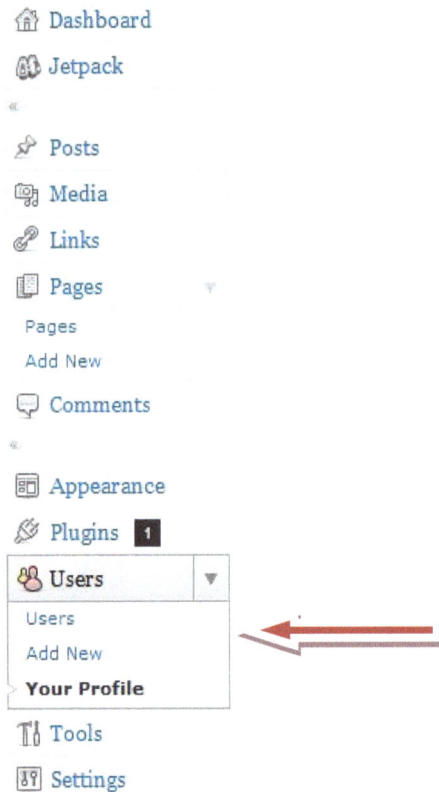

2. Click on "Your Profile" from the "Users" drop down menu, as shown below:

3. Clicking on "Your Profile" in the "Users" drop down menu, gives you the following page, where you can set up your proofreading options – a good thing to do if you make typos like me!

Part 3 - Adding E-Commerce
We are now going to add a free store to your suite. This is done via plugins!

Step 10 – Installing the ecwid plugin

1. Click "Plugins" on the Dashboard left-side menu bar, as shown below:

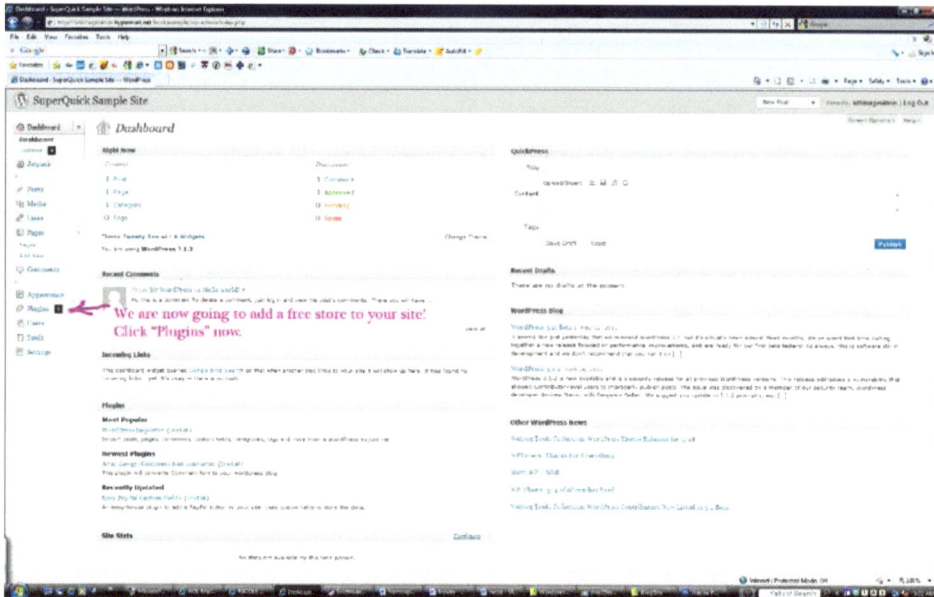

2. Click "Add New" as shown below:

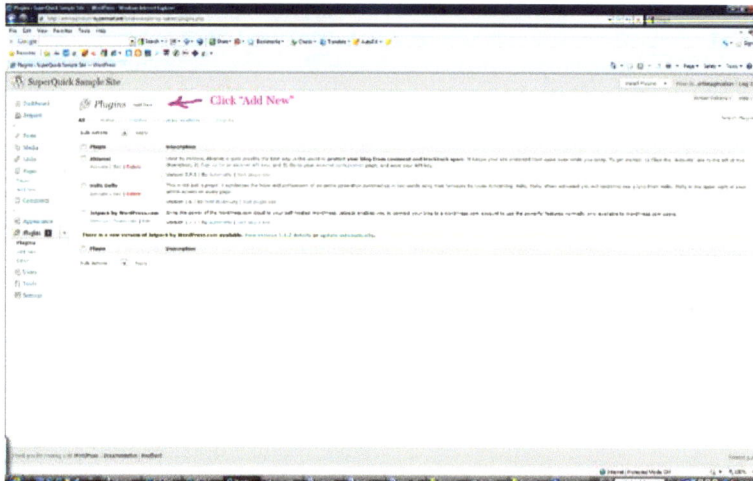

3. *In search box type "ecwid" and then click "Search Plugins" button as shown below:*

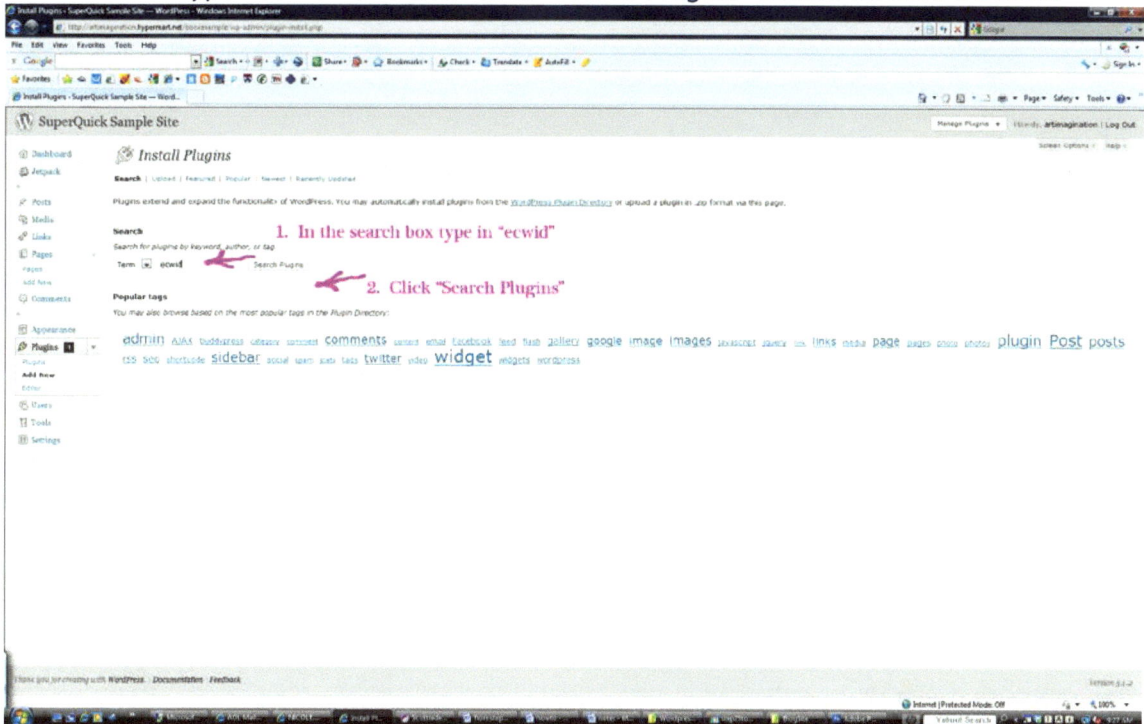

4. *When the "Ecwid Shopping Cart" appears below, click "Install Now" as shown below:*

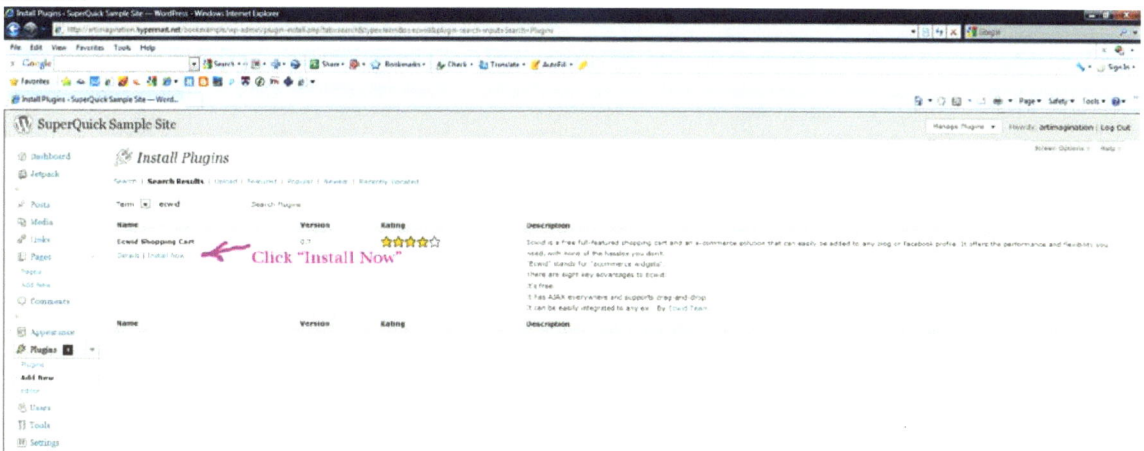

5. *Click "Activate Plugin"*

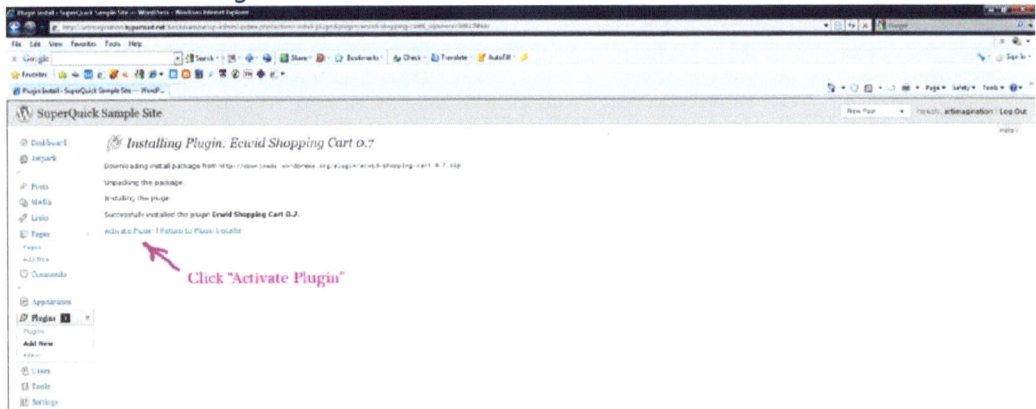

6. *When the ecwid plugin is activated, your plugin page will now look like the screen capture shown below:*

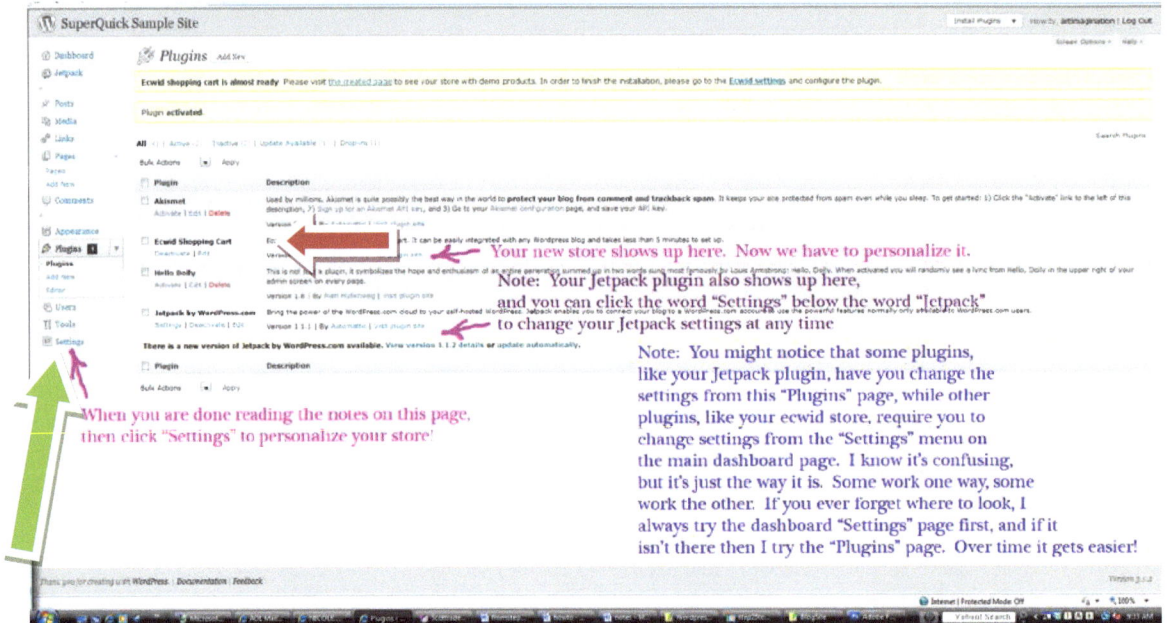

The ecwid plugin, which is the foundation for your new store, shows up where the red arrow is above.

7. *Click the "Settings" menu (see the green arrow above) to personalize your store!*

8. Click "Ecwid shopping cart" from the "Settings Menu as shown enlarged below:

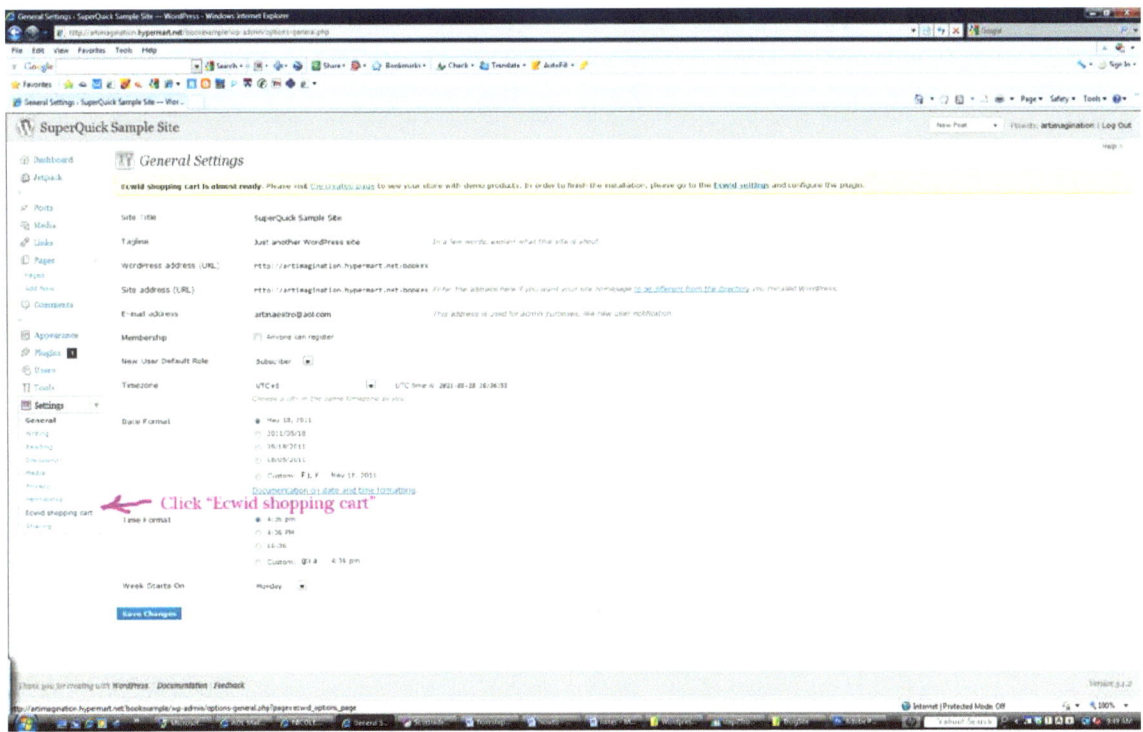

9. *Clicking "Ecwid shopping cart" from the "Settings" menu (as shown above) will give you the following screen, called the "Ecwid settings page."   This Ecwid settings page is where you can choose how many rows and columns of products show up in your store. You can use the default numbers for now.*

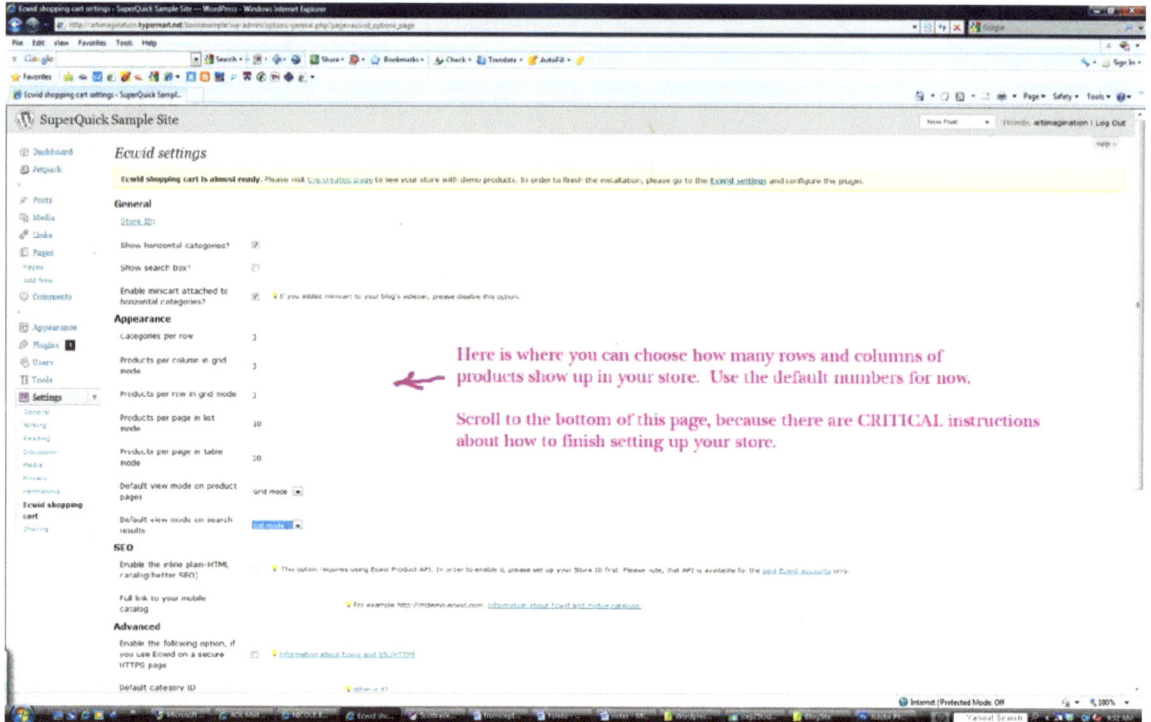

Here is where you can choose how many rows and columns of products show up in your store. Use the default numbers for now.

Scroll to the bottom of this page, because there are CRITICAL instructions about how to finish setting up your store.

1. **Scroll to the bottom of this Ecwid settings page, because there are CRITICAL instructions there about how you are to finish setting up your store.**
   Here is what you will see at the bottom of the Ecwid settings page:

Follow the instructions at the bottom of your Ecwid settings page to go on to the next step. What the instructions at the bottom of your (and the above) Ecwid settings page will tell you to do as follows:

   a. Open this URL: https://my.ecwid.com/cp/#register. NOTE: open this new URL in an entirely new browser window – you do not wish to close your main site Dashboard yet.

When you open a new internet browser window and paste in the https://my.ecwid.com/cp/#register URL, then you will get to the 'Sign In or Register' form, as shown below:

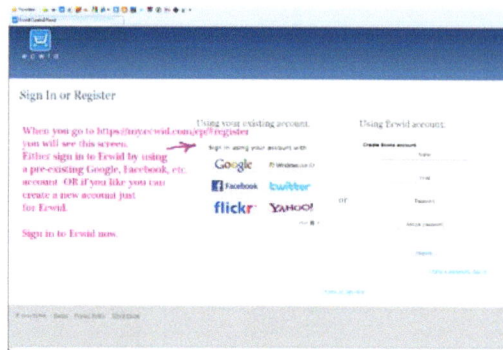

•Now you need to register an account at Ecwid. Use section "Using Ecwid account" for that. The registration is free.
Alternatively to registering an entirely new account at Ecwid, at this point you can alternatively log into Ecwid using your account at Gmail, Facebook, Twitter, Yahoo, or another provider. Choose one from the list of the providers (click on 'More providers' if you don't see your provider there).   Click on the provider logo, you will be redirected to the account login page.
Submit your username/password there to login to your Ecwid.

Note: the login might take several seconds. Please, be patient.

b. *Once login to ecwid is complete, you will see your Ecwid Dashboard, as shown below:*

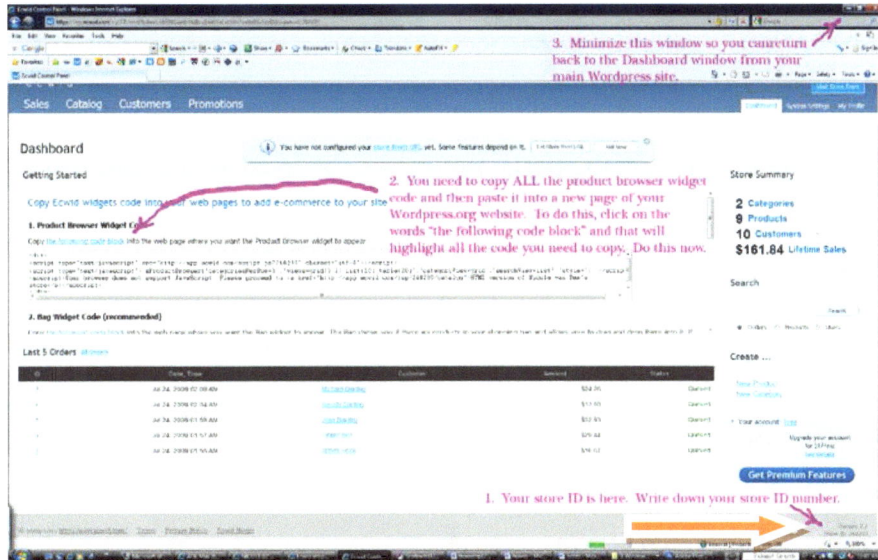

The above screen capture shows the resulting Ecwid Store Dashboard page – this is the design and implementation space for YOUR online e-Commerce store.

NOTE: You now have TWO "dashboards" open – you have this new ecwid store dashboard page open, and in addition you still have the original Wordpress Dashboard open. Remember that the original Wordpress dashboard is the dashboard for your main Wordpress site. The ecwid store dashboard is the dashboard solely for your ecwid ecommerce shopping part of your site. The next steps deal with your ecwid store dashboard, not the main Wordpress site dashboard.

• Look at the right bottom corner of the resulting Ecwid Store dashboard page - You will see I drew an ➡ pointing to the "Store ID: NNNNNN" text, where NNNNNN is your Store ID. That is the Store ID for your store – nobody else has the same ID number. For example if the text you see in the bottom right corner is Store ID: 981003, then your Store ID is 981003. WRITE DOWN AND SAVE YOUR STORE ID – YOU WILL NEED IT! You will also get your Store ID by email.

c. *Also on this ecwid store dashboard page you will see "Product Browser Widget Code" shown by the pink arrow below.*

Getting Started

Copy Ecwid widgets code into ~~your~~ web pages to add e-commerce to your site

1. Product Browser Widget Code

Copy the following code block into the web page where you want the Product Browser widget to appear.

```
<div>
<script type='text/javascript' src='http://app.ecwid.com/script.js?248230' charset='utf-8'></script>
<script type='text/javascript'> xProductBrowser("categoriesPerRow=3","views=grid(3,3) list(10) table(20)","categoryView=grid","searchView=list","style="); </script
<noscript>Your browser does not support JavaScript. Please proceed to <a href='http://app.ecwid.com/jsp/248230/catalog'>HTML version of Nicole van Dea's
store</a></noscript>
</div>
```

2. You need to copy ALL the product browser widget code and then paste it into a new page of your Wordpress.org website. To do this, click on the words "the following code block" and that will highlight all the code you need to copy. Do this now.

d. You need to copy ALL the "product browser widget" code and then paste it into a new page of your Wordpress.org website. To do this, click on the words "the following code block" (shown by the pink arrow above) and that will automatically highlight all the code you need to copy. Do this now.

2. In your internet browser, minimize this ecwid store dashboard window in the usual way, by clicking the dash (see green arrow below to remind you how to minimize a screen without closing it):

By minimizing the ecwid store dashboard page, you can return back to the main Wordpress Dashboard window that is the Dashboard for your main Wordpress site.

3. SUMMARY: We have now installed ecwid as a plugin, and begun to set up the store using the ecwid dashboard. However, we still need to create a page on Wordpress that will have your new store on it! We set up the page to house your new store in the next chapter.

Step 11 – Adding a New Page to Your Wordpress Site

1. *We are now going to add an entirely new page to your Wordpress website. The purpose of this page is to have your new ecwid store showing on it!*

2. *When we minimized the ecwid store dashboard, we returned to the Wordpress dashboard, still open to the Ecwid settings page. Click on the "Pages" menu, shown by the pink arrow below.*

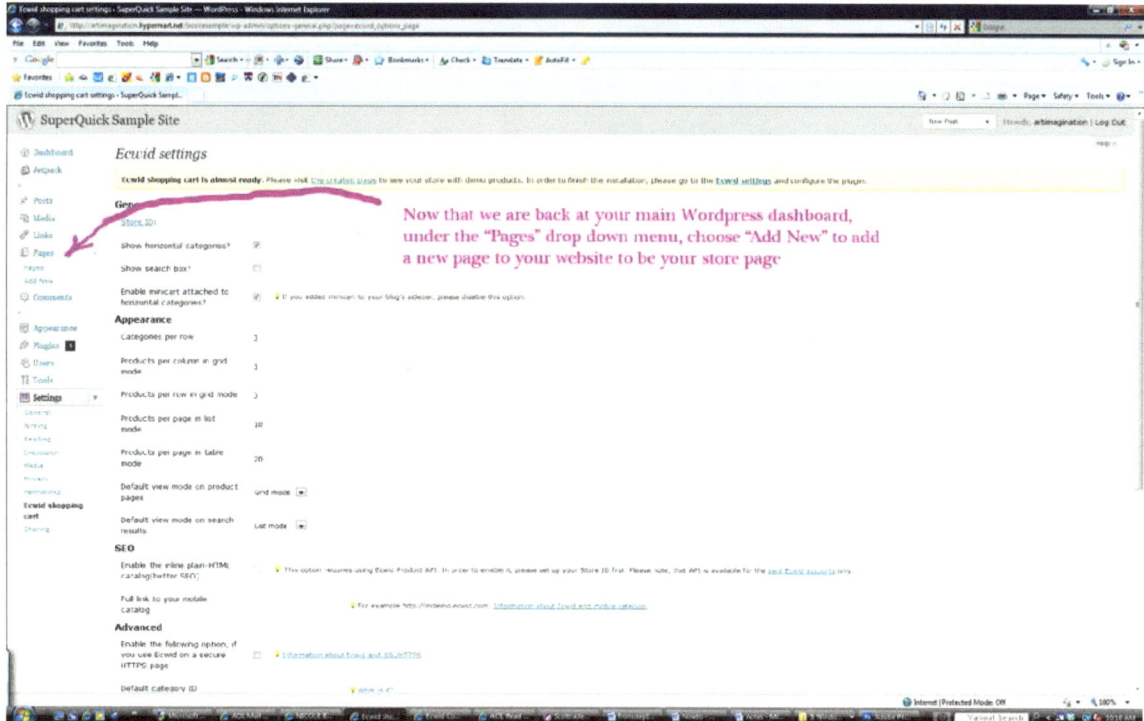

Here is an enlargement of the "Pages" drop down menu. Click on "Add New" as shown below:

3. *This brings us to a screen "Add New Page" that lets us customize a new page. You can give it any title, add any html, etc.*

4. In this example, we are going to make a new page specifically for your ecwid store. Do the following steps, also shown below:

a. Type in the name for your store (see the _green arrow_ below);

b. Click html (see _red arrow_) – this will bring you to the place where you can paste in the "product browser widget" code that you just copied in the prior chapter from the ecwid store dashboard page.

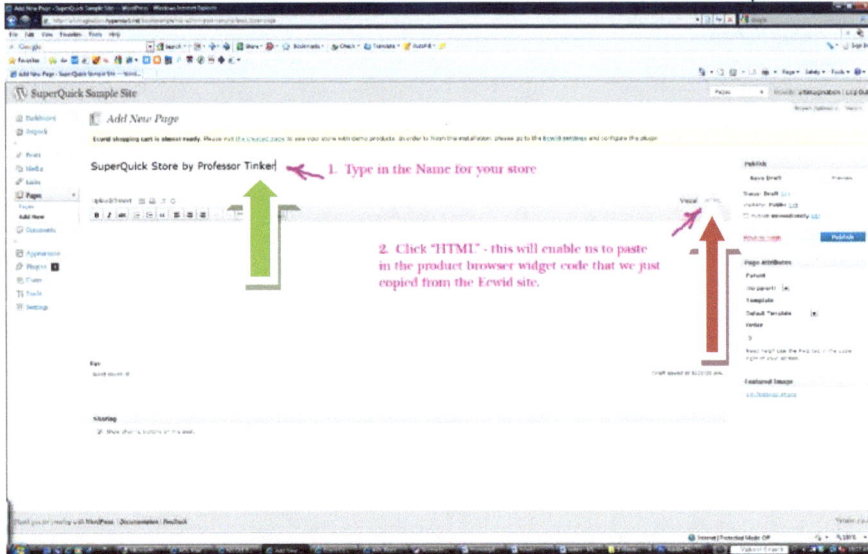

c. Click your cursor in the text box, as shown by the _orange arrow_ below, and paste your "product browser widget" code into the html text box now, then click the blue "Publish" box (shown by the _blue arrow_ below):

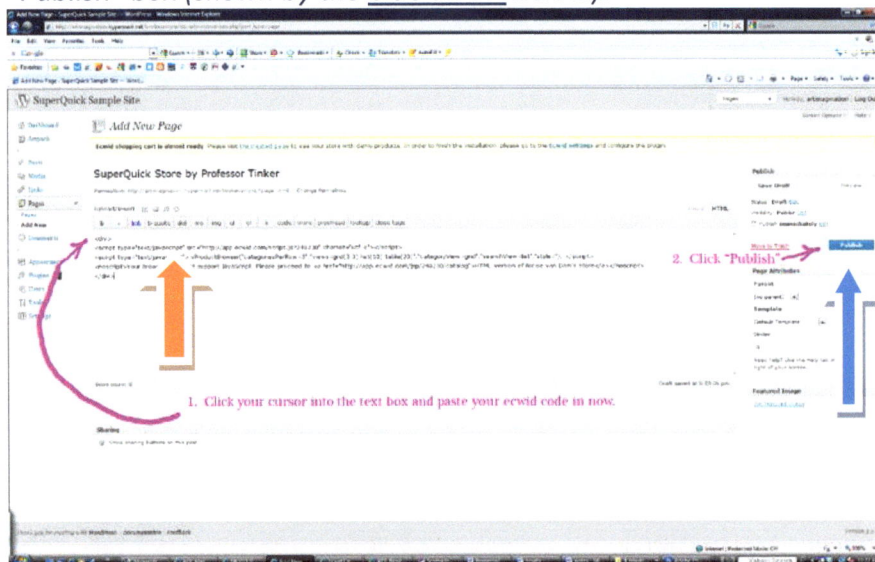

5. Click "View Page" as shown below to see your progress:

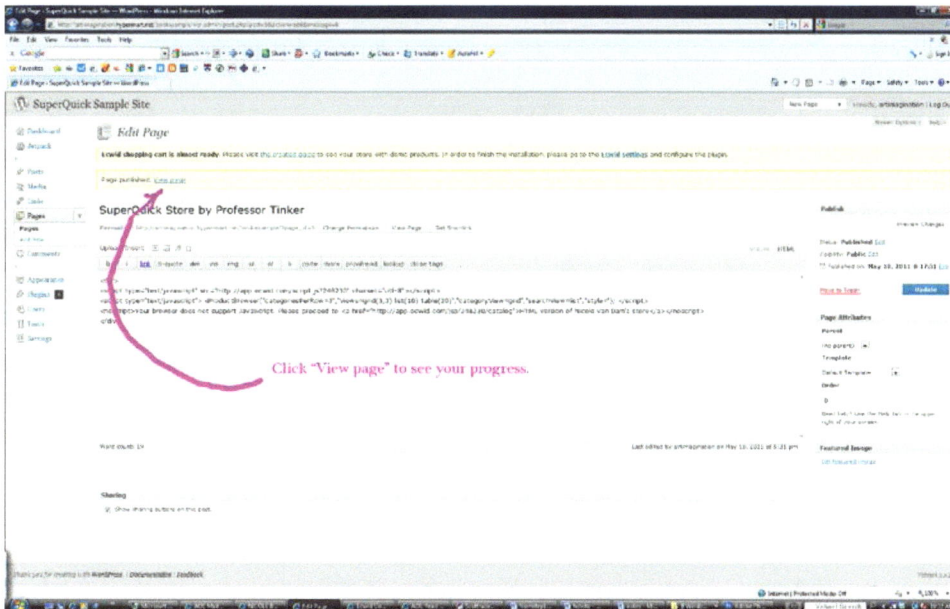

Click "View page" to see your progress.

6. —And what you will see is the following webpage on your site that has your store, with the default store products that ecwid provides. We will put in your own store products later. Note your store shows up on the menu bar under the header as well.

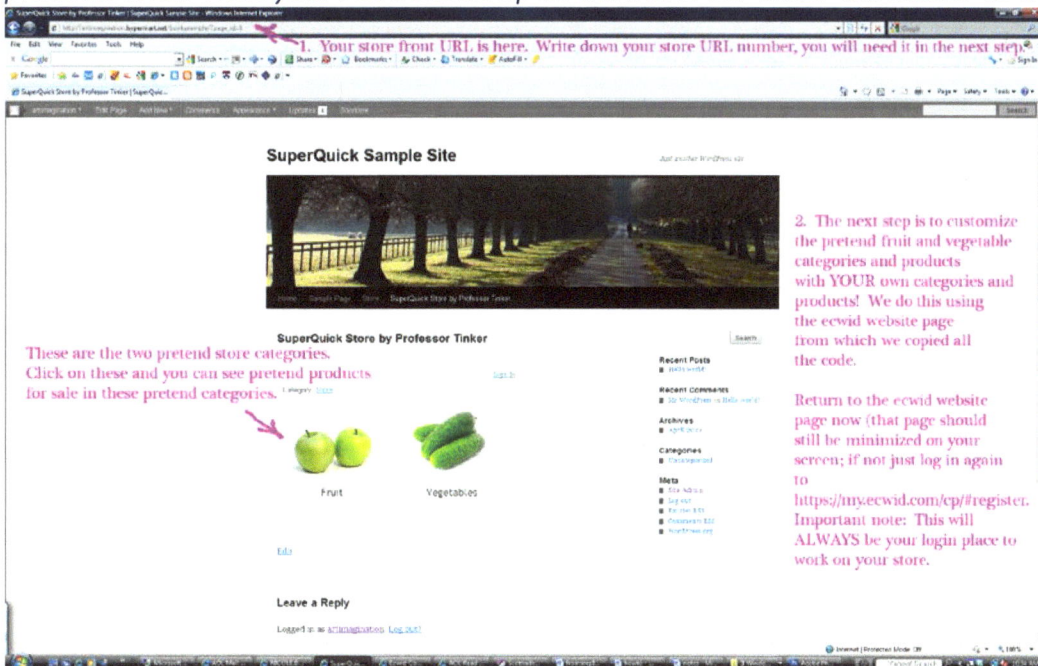

1. Your store front URL is here. Write down your store URL number, you will need it in the next step.

SuperQuick Sample Site

Just another WordPress site

SuperQuick Store by Professor Tinker

These are the two pretend store categories.
Click on these and you can see pretend products
for sale in these pretend categories.

Fruit   Vegetables

Edit

2. The next step is to customize the pretend fruit and vegetable categories and products with YOUR own categories and products! We do this using the ecwid website page from which we copied all the code.

Return to the ecwid website page now (that page should still be minimized on your screen; if not just log in again to https://my.ecwid.com/cp/#register. Important note: This will ALWAYS be your login place to work on your store.

Leave a Reply

Logged in as artimagination. Log out?

7. Make note of your store front URL – see the orange arrow below to find it:

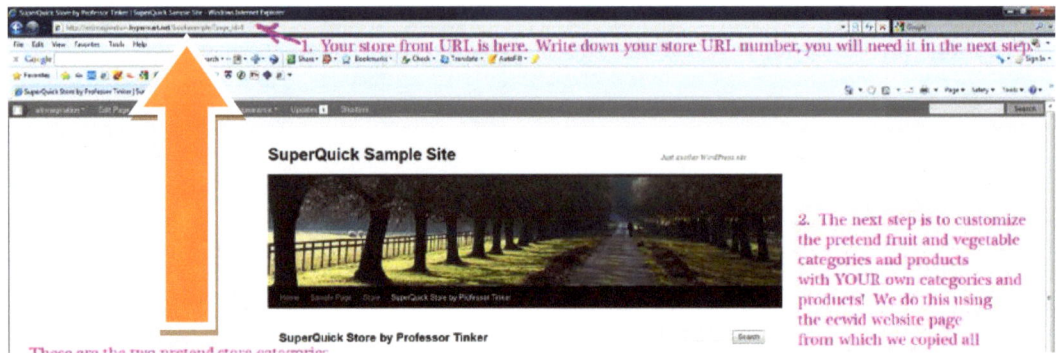

NOTE: Step 15 of this Book goes into more detail regarding adding Pages to your Wordpress site, so if you need more information on adding Pages, you will find it in Step 15 of this book.

The next step is to customize the pretend fruit and vegetable categories and products with YOUR own categories and products! We do this using the ecwid website page from which we copied all the code.

Return to the ecwid website page now (that page should still be minimized on your screen; if not just log in again to https://my.ecwid.com/cp/#register. Important note: This will ALWAYS be your login place to work on your store.

STEP 12 – Finishing Setting up the Store Back-End
(Payment, Shipping, etc.)

1. The next step is to customize the pretend fruit and vegetable categories and products with YOUR own categories and products! We do this using the ecwid website page from which we copied all the code.

2. Return to the ecwid store dashboard page now (that page should still be minimized on your screen; if not just log in again to https://my.ecwid.com/cp/#register.

   Important note: https://my.ecwid.com/cp/#register will ALWAYS be your login place to work on your store.

3. ADD YOUR STOREFRONT URL THAT YOU WROTE DONW IN STEP 7 ABOVE TO THE ECWID DASHBOARD PAGE, AS SHOWN BELOW:

   -Click "Set Store front URL" as shown by the pink arrow below:

-Type in all the information you have in the next screen, as shown below. This information includes your store name, and you can even upload a photo for your invoices!

-Make sure you type in your storefront URL where the orange arrow ⬆ is below:

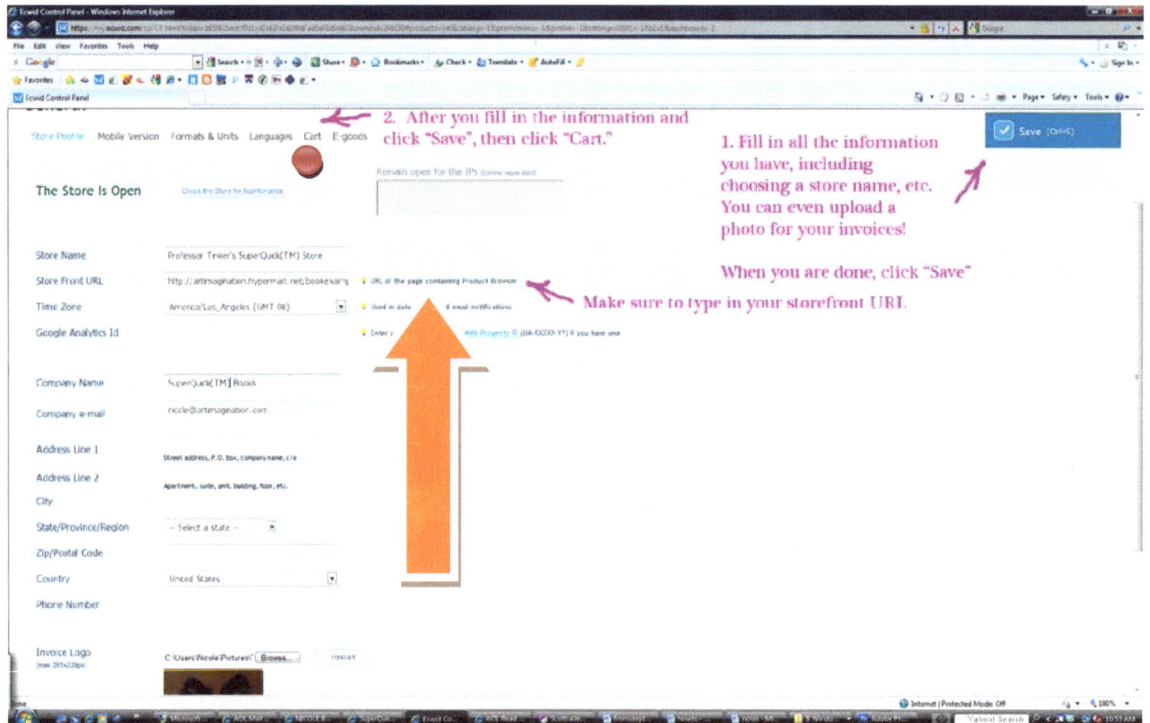

-When you are done, click the blue "Save" button in the upper right corner (see above).

-Next. Click "Cart" (see ⬤ above to find the "Cart" on the upper menu)

8. This brings you to the following screen:

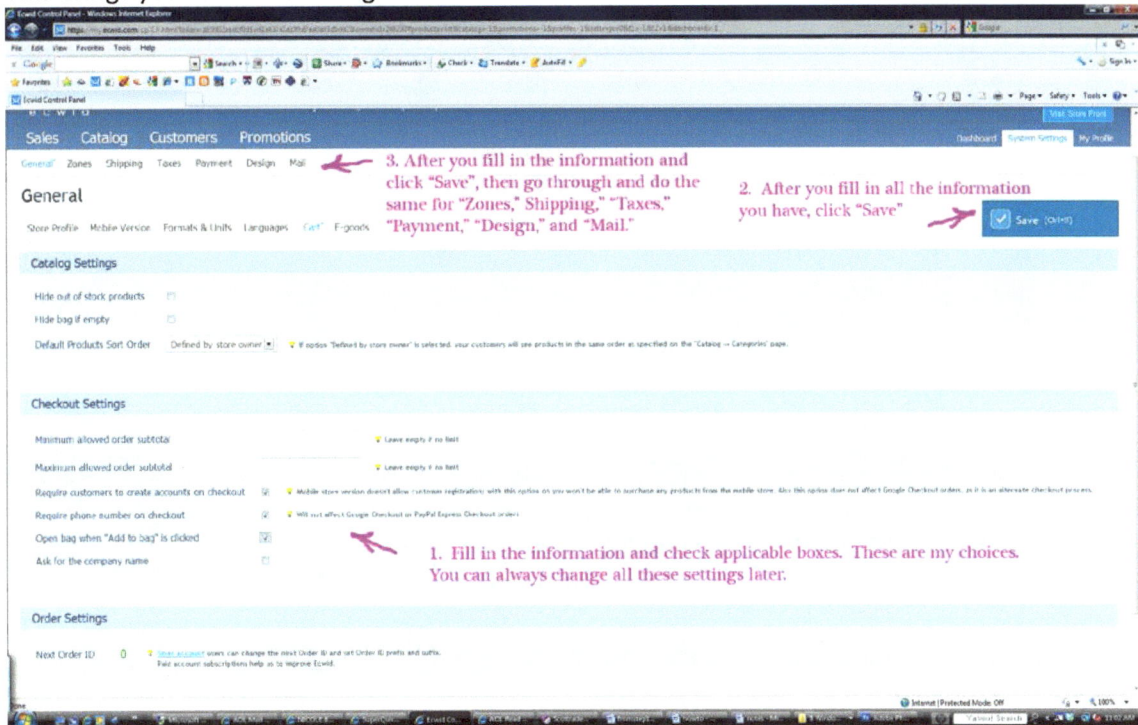

-Fill in the information requested and check the applicable boxes. You can see my choices above – yours may differ. You can change these settings later.

-After you fill in all the information you can, click the blue save button in the upper right corner.

-After you click "save" as set forth above, then go through each of the tabs for "Zones," "Shipping," "Taxes," Payment", "Design," and "Mail" and fill in the information for each of those. Your information will depend on your business, your preferences, and your geographic location.

   EXAMPLES OF MY CHOICES:

9. **SETTING UP SHIPPING**:
   I chose to use the US Postal Service (USPS), so here is how I set that up:
   When you choose USPS, they will ask you for a USPS Web Tools ID – don't worry – you get that from setting up a USPS account with the United States Postal Service, and there is

more info on that at http://kb.ecwid.com/USPS :

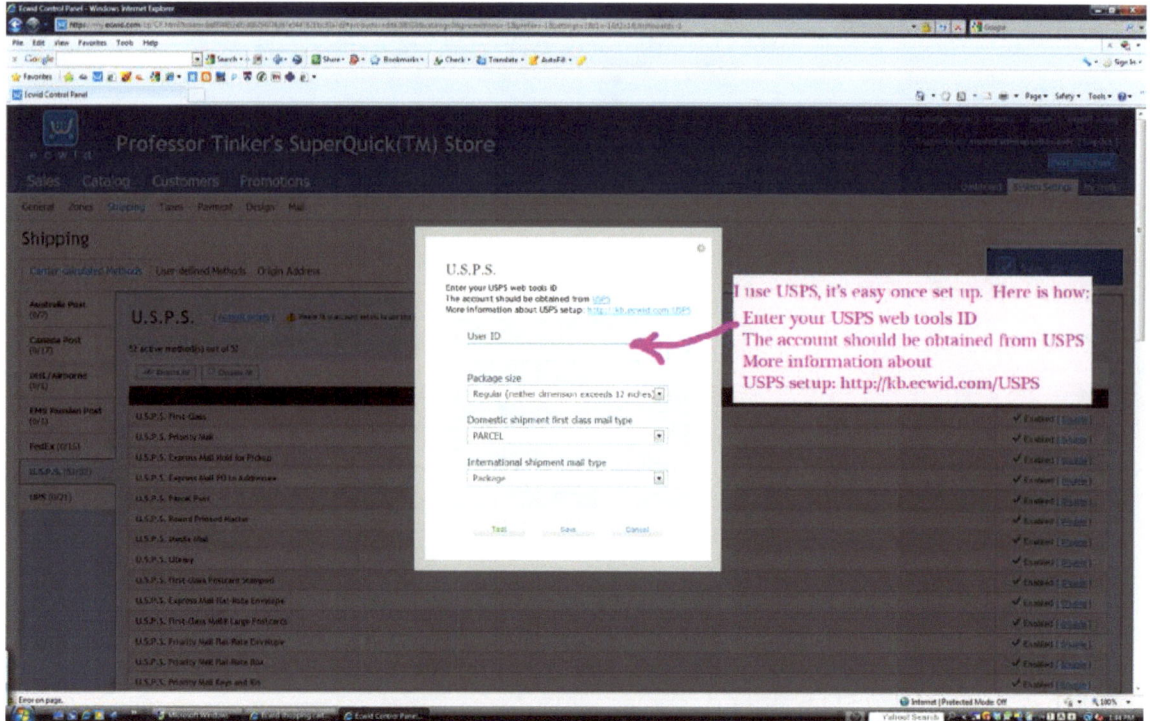

Enlargement of the main part of the above screen capture – in the enlargement you can see the hyperlinks so setting everything up is pretty straightforward:

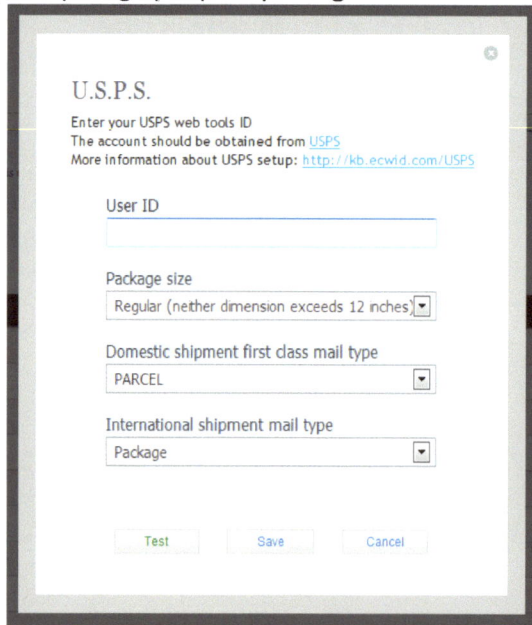

U.S.P.S.

Enter your USPS web tools ID
The account should be obtained from USPS
More information about USPS setup: http://kb.ecwid.com/USPS

User ID

Package size
Regular (nether dimension exceeds 12 inches)

Domestic shipment first class mail type
PARCEL

International shipment mail type
Package

Test   Save   Cancel

Once you put in your user ID in the prior screen, just follow the steps, as follows:

1. Click add country to add destinations you will deal with in your store

2. Choose the countries, click Add.

Under the Shipping menu, I use USPS as my choice, Enable all the types of delivery services you wish to use to fulfill orders.

Make sure to click "Save" when you are done.

MAKE SURE TO ALWAYS CLICK SAVE AS YOU WORK AND WHEN YOU ARE DONE, SO YOU DON'T LOSE YOUR WORK.

EXAMPLES OF MY CHOICES 2:

10. **SETTING UP PAYMENT MECHANISM**:

Click through the various menu tabs as shown below. Make sure you go through each payment method.

NOTE: If you haven't already signed up for a free Google Checkout account and a free Paypal account, you might wish to do so - that way you can easily receive payments by either Paypal or Google checkout - in other words,
customers will have more choices of how to pay when they use your store.

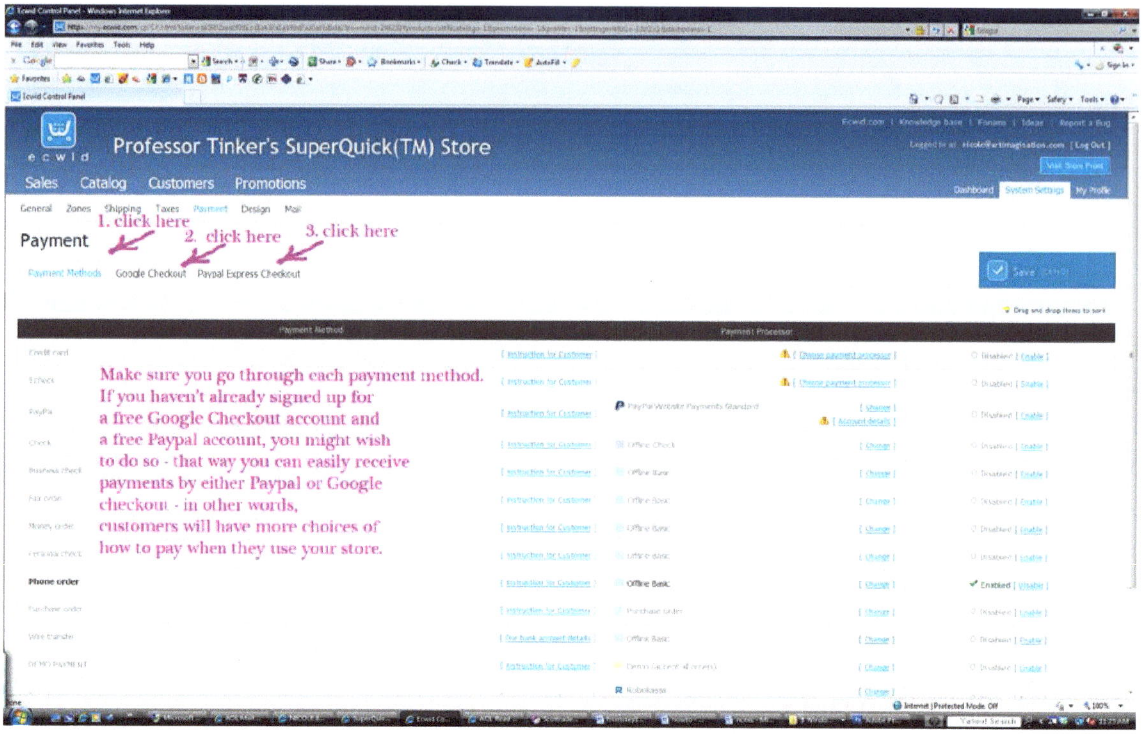

MAKE SURE TO ALWAYS CLICK SAVE AS YOU WORK AND WHEN YOU ARE DONE, SO YOU DON'T LOSE YOUR WORK.

11. More on Navigating through your Ecwid Store Dashboard – the Sales Tab:
What the Sales Tab shows you:

If you click on the Sales Tab, it will show you pretend orders. Once your store is up and running, you will see real orders here!

Step 13 - Adding Your Own Products to Your Store

First click the "Catalog" tab as shown by the pink arrows below:

The Catalog work area is where you will go to add products to your store.

    a. *The first step to adding products to your store is to decide what categories those products belong in. For example, a blouse might belong in the Clothing category while this SuperQuick™ Wordpress how-to book and my SuperQuick™ Facebook how-to book might belong in a "SuperQuick™ How-To Books" category. How you define the categories is up to you.*

    b. *As shown in the illustration below, fill in the name of your category - I chose "SuperQuick (TM) How-To Books" as the name for my new category. I also uploaded a photo of one of my SuperQuick (TM) books. Please do the same for the first category you wish to add, then click "Save."*

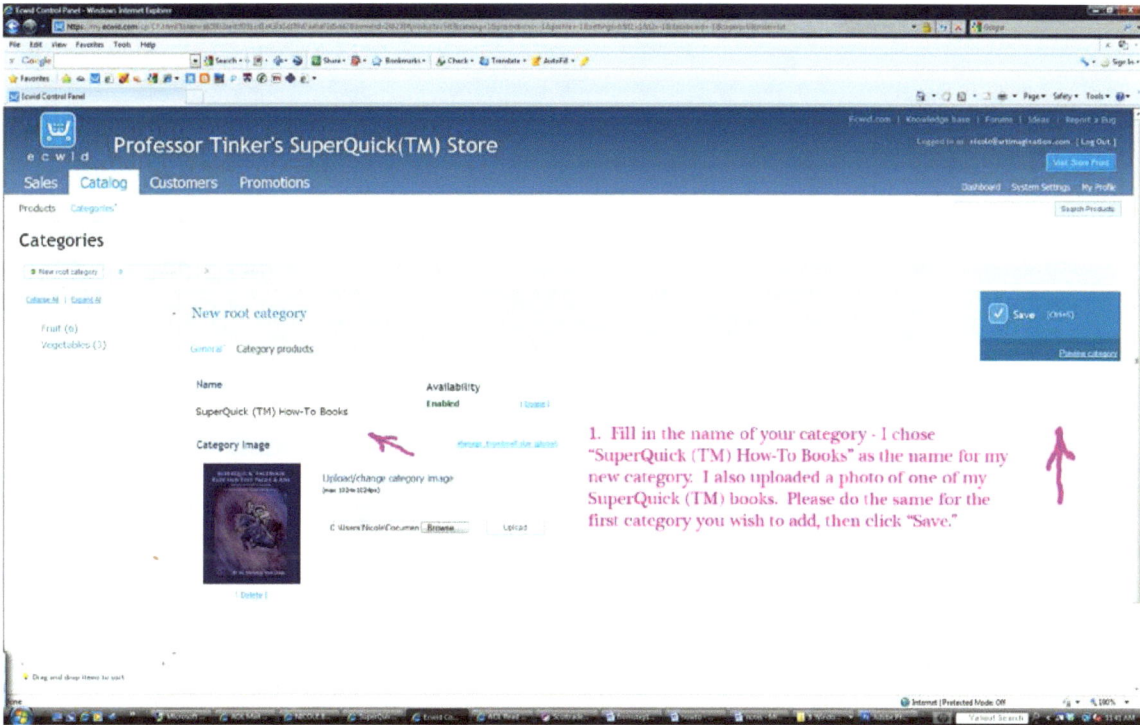

1. Fill in the name of your category - I chose "SuperQuick (TM) How-To Books" as the name for my new category. I also uploaded a photo of one of my SuperQuick (TM) books. Please do the same for the first category you wish to add, then click "Save."

c. The next step is to click "Category products" as shown below, to add the specific products that are for sale in the category you just added:

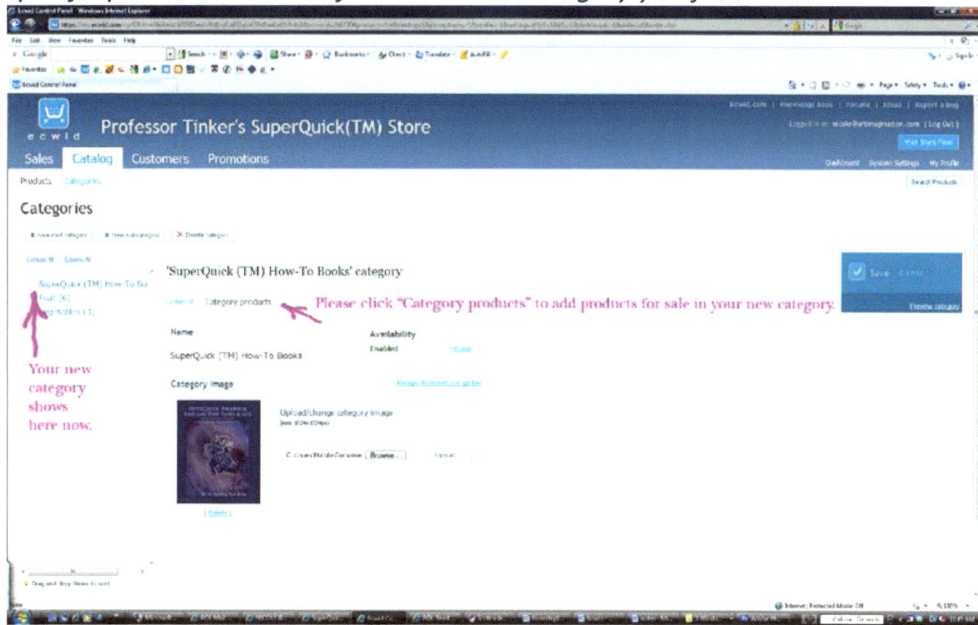

Your new category shows here now.

Please click "Category products" to add products for sale in your new category.

d. The click "Add Products" as shown below:

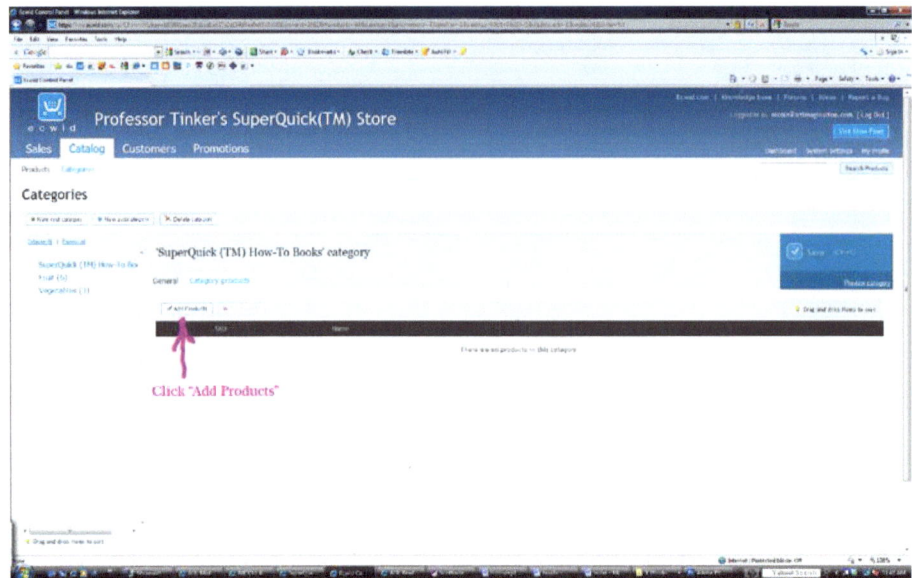

e. Then click "Products" as shown below:

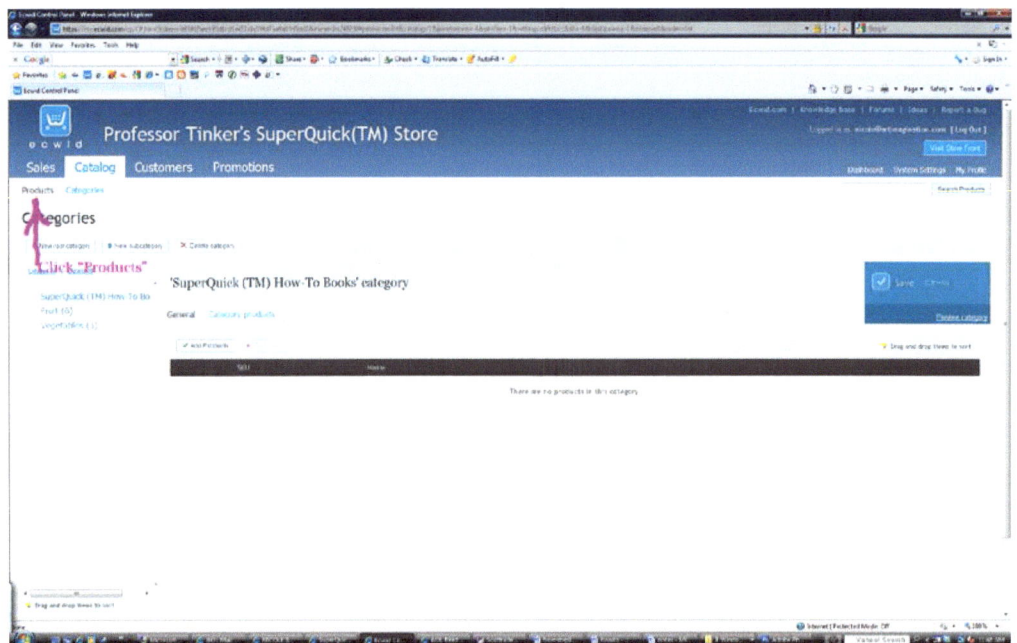

f. Then click "New Products" to FINALLY add one of your products:

NOTE: You can have up to 100 products for free (without paying for ecwid). Different variations (such as different sizes of shirt) of the same products still counts as only one products of the 100, so actually the 100 products is generous.

Clicking "New Products" as shown above will bring you to the following screen.

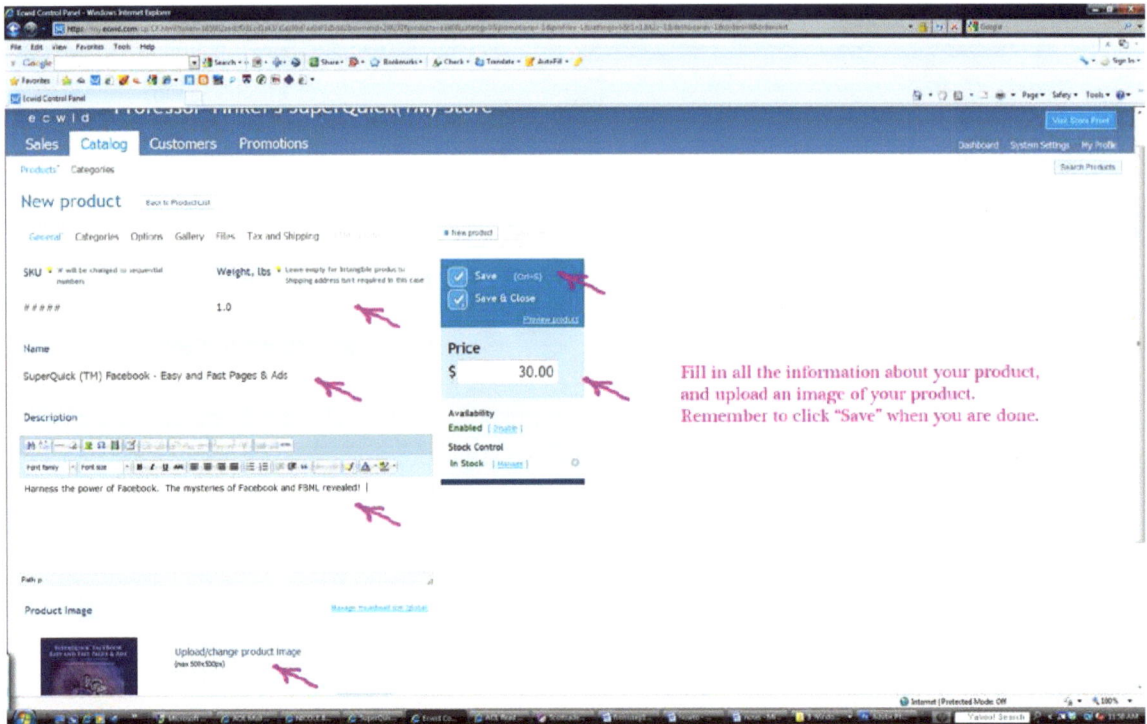

Once you are at this screen, to add your products, simply fill in all the information about your product, as shown by the pink arrows below, and upload an image of your product (remember 4" images of 72dpi -150 dpi is more than large enough for this purpose on the web).

Remember to click Save after each product to save that product.

NEXT CLICK CATEGORIES (as shown below):

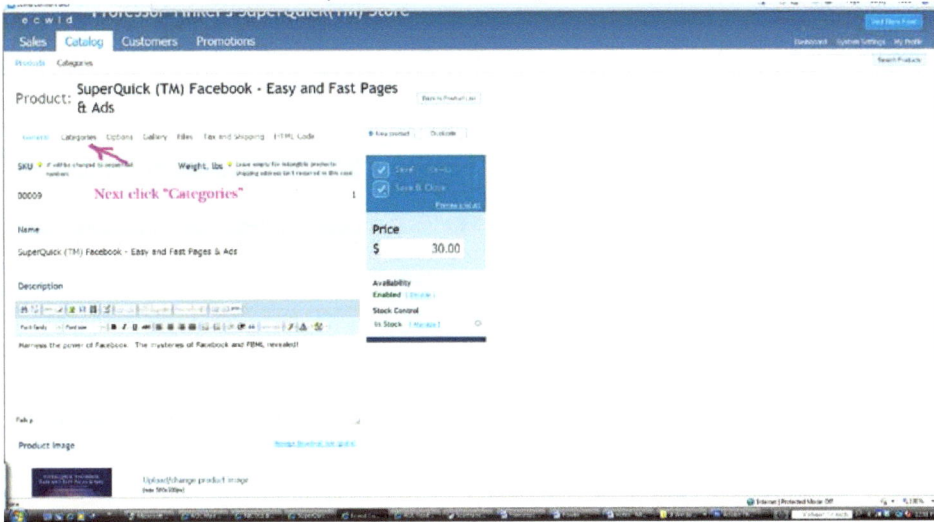

NOW THAT YOU HAVE CREATED YOUR NEW PRODUCT, SAVED IT, AND CLICKED THE CATEGORIES PAGE (AS SHOWN ABOVE), WHEN YOU ARE ON THE CATEGORIES PAGE YOU NEED TO:

1. *PUT A CHECKMARK IN THE CHECKBOX FOR THE CATEGORY TO WHICH YOUR PRODUCT BELONGS; THEN*
2. *CLICK "SAVE"*
3. *NEXT CLICK OPTIONS (all as shown below):*

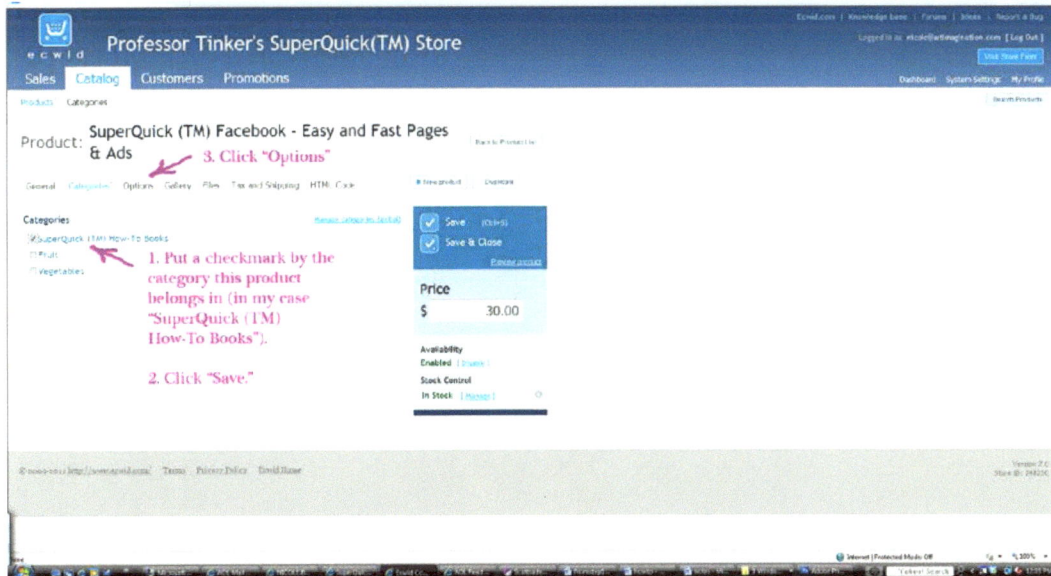

Now that you are in the Options menu, you will find the amazing power behind this ecwid store engine.

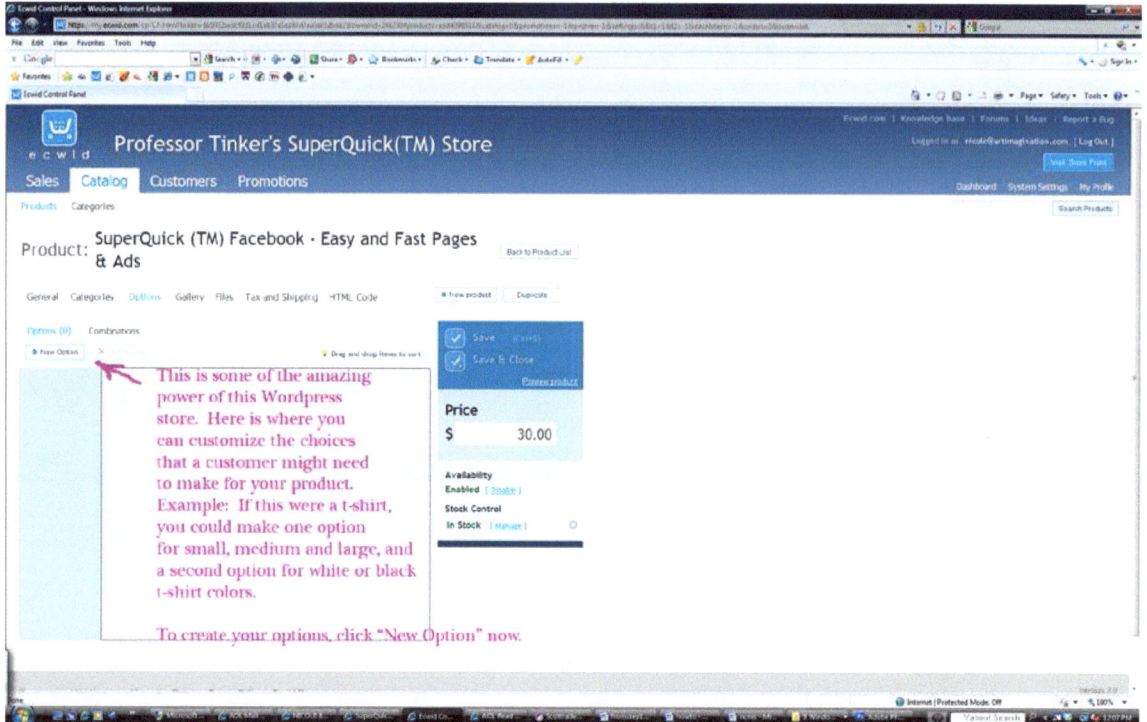

The "Options" tab provides some of the amazing customization power of this Wordpress store. The "Options" tab is where you can customize the choices that a customer might need to make for your product. Example: If this were a t-shirt, you could make one option for small, medium and large, and a second option for white or black t-shirt colors. All this together still only counts as one product of your free 100 products.

To create your options, click "New Option" now.

74

Once you click "New Option" this is what you do, as shown pictorially through the pink numbers below:

1. Click "New Selection"
2. Pick how your customer sees his choices. I picked "radio buttons" - you can always change your choices.
3. Fill in the information for each new selection you create (for example, any changes to the base price of the item resulting from a customer selecting a particular option is inserted here).
4. Click Save
5. After you click "Save" then click "New Option" and you can repeat list of 5 items over again for each option you wish to create for that product.

6. When you are through setting up your options, click Save
7. After you click "Save" click "View Store Front" so you can see your progress.

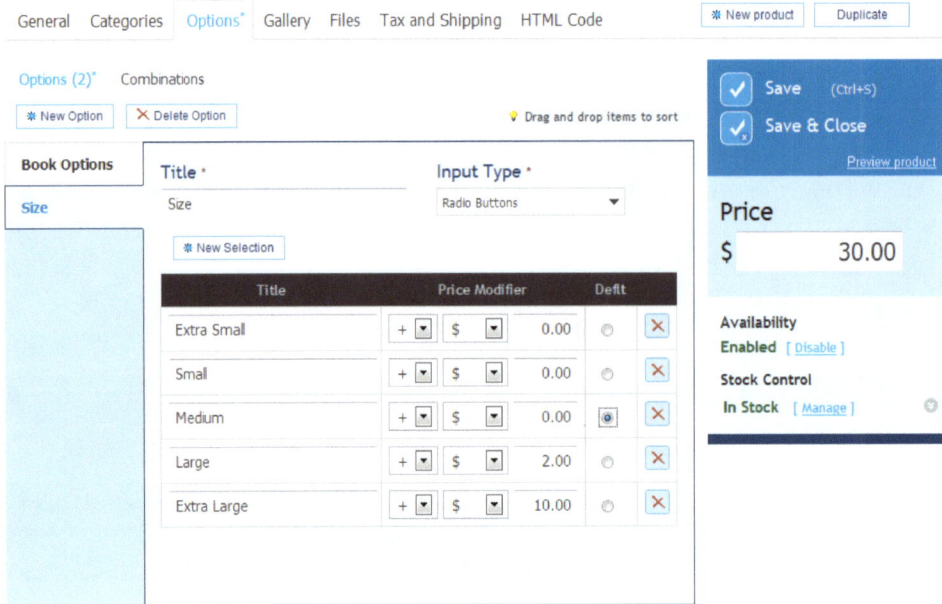

Above is a close-up of what you might set up as size options for a clothing product.
In the above example, I chose to use radial buttons to set this up, and if you look you will see that "Medium" is the default size.

Below is the screen capture from which this close-up came.

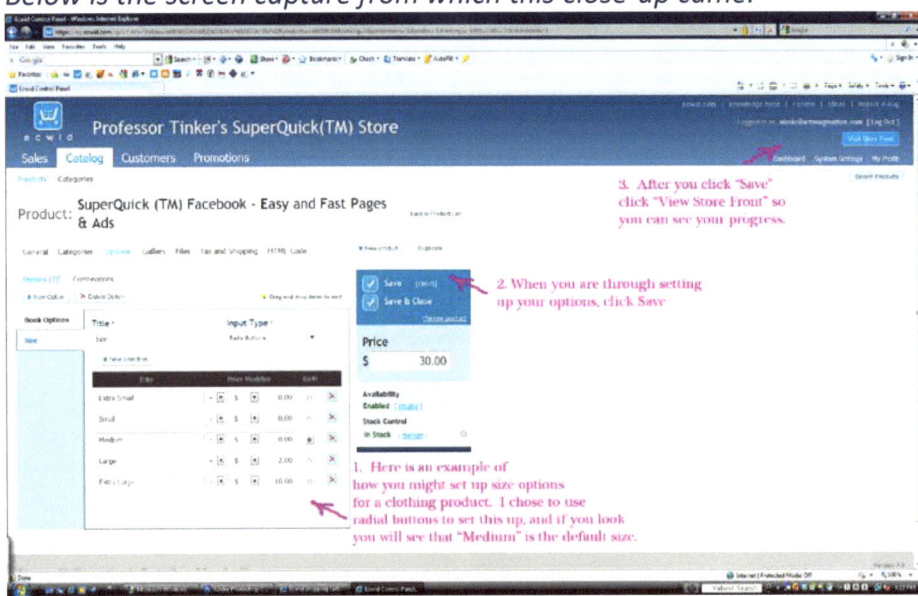

After you

When you are through with your options and click "Save," as previously stated you can then click "View Store Front" so you can see your progress:

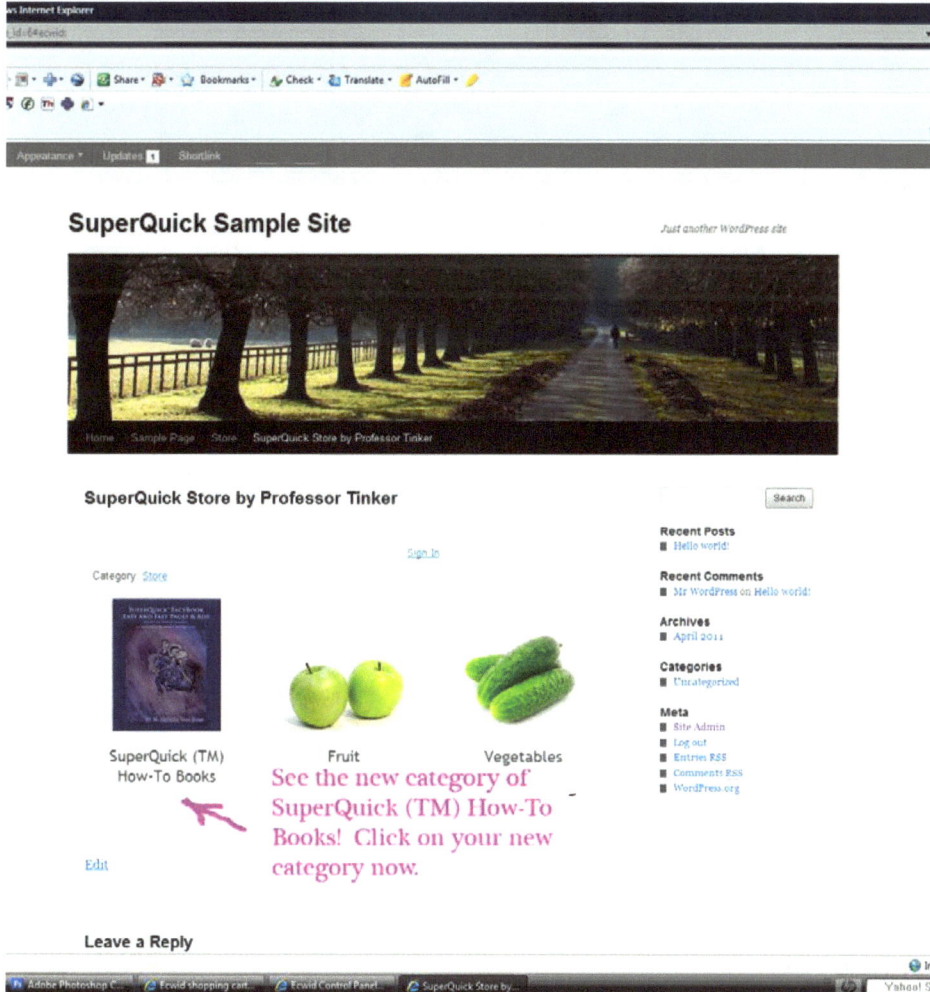

See the new category above of SuperQuick (TM) How-To Books! Remember that the fruits and vegetables categories are the original default categories that automatically come with ecwid — you can remove the fruits and vegetables categories (or any other category) by using the Category menu in the ecwid store dashboard to remove them.

You can click on your new category now to test it!

Below is the new product I added to my new SuperQuick™ How-To Books category. Click on you new product now, to see how the options you chose look!

Here is the new product we added to the new category. Click on the new product now, to see how the options we chose look!

Here is the new book product with the options I chose. In the close-up you can see the options I chose was signing, size and gift wrapping. I did the size in this example solely so you could see how the size choices look. Since in real life, there aren't size choices for books so I will eventually eliminate these:

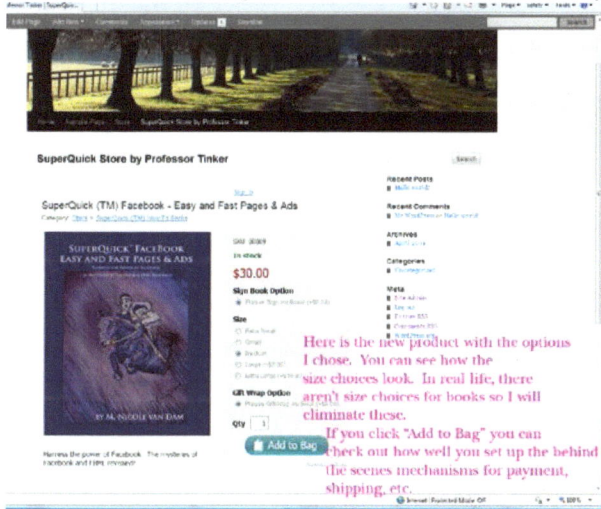

SKU 00009

In stock

$30.00

Sign Book Option
◉ Please Sign my Book! (+$5.00)

Size
○ Extra Small
○ Small
◉ Medium
○ Large (+$2.00)
○ Extra Large (+$10.00)

Gift Wrap Option
◉ Please GiftWrap my Book (+$8.00)

Qty 1

🛍 Add to Bag

CLOSEUP UP OF HOW OPTIONS LOOK IN THE STORE:

If you click "Add to Bag" then you can test how well you set up the behind the scenes mechanisms for payment, shipping, etc.

CONGRATULATIONS ON YOUR NEW FUNCTIONING STORE!

Part 4 – Posting to Your Wordpress Blog, Adding More Pages and Creating a Custom Menu under Your Image Header

Step 14 - Posting to Your Wordpress Blog

The very first page Wordpress automatically by default creates for you is actually a blog page. Blogs are great to build and maintain community for your business. In this step 14, we will show you how to actually add and classify your own posts on your blog page.

1. *Click on "Posts" in your Wordpress dashboard left side menu bar. This brings you to a dropdown menu, as shown below. Click "Add New" in the "Posts" dropdown menu, as shown below:*

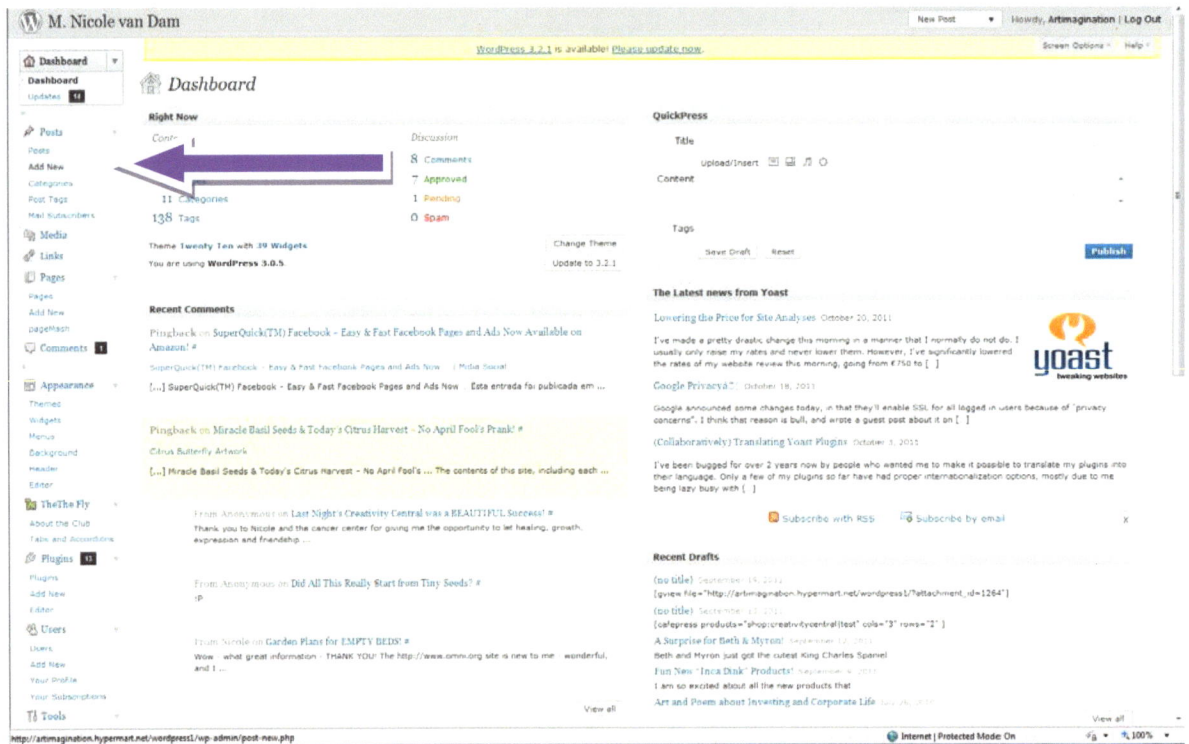

2. As shown below:

Type in the title for the post you are making;

Type in the content of the post itself, in the content box.
In typing content, please note the following:

If you have html selected at the HTML tab for the content box, then you can type in html here as well. Many sites on the web, such as quackit.com, provide free html code for you to copy and paste.

By clicking the icons above the content box, where it says "Upload/Insert", then you can insert photos, video, music, etc. into your post.

In "Categories portion of this workspace you can also choose a category to classify your post. If you don't have the category created yet that you would want to choose, all you have to do to create a category is to click "Add New Categories" in the "Categories" area, as shown by the

If you decide to install the "Yoast Wordpress SEO" plugin, you can manage search engine optimization for each blog post here as well. See Part 5 of this book for more info on advanced plugins and widgets.

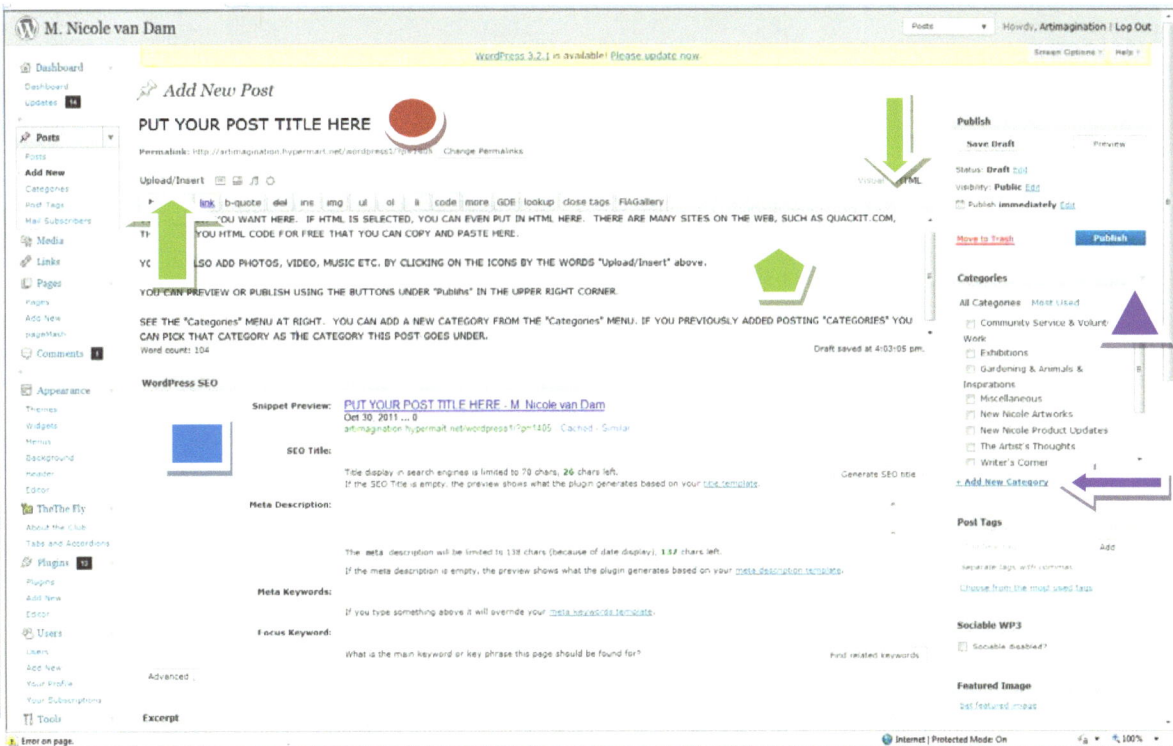

3. You can also manage and create new Categories for your posts by clicking "Categories" in the "Pages" drop down menu, as shown below:

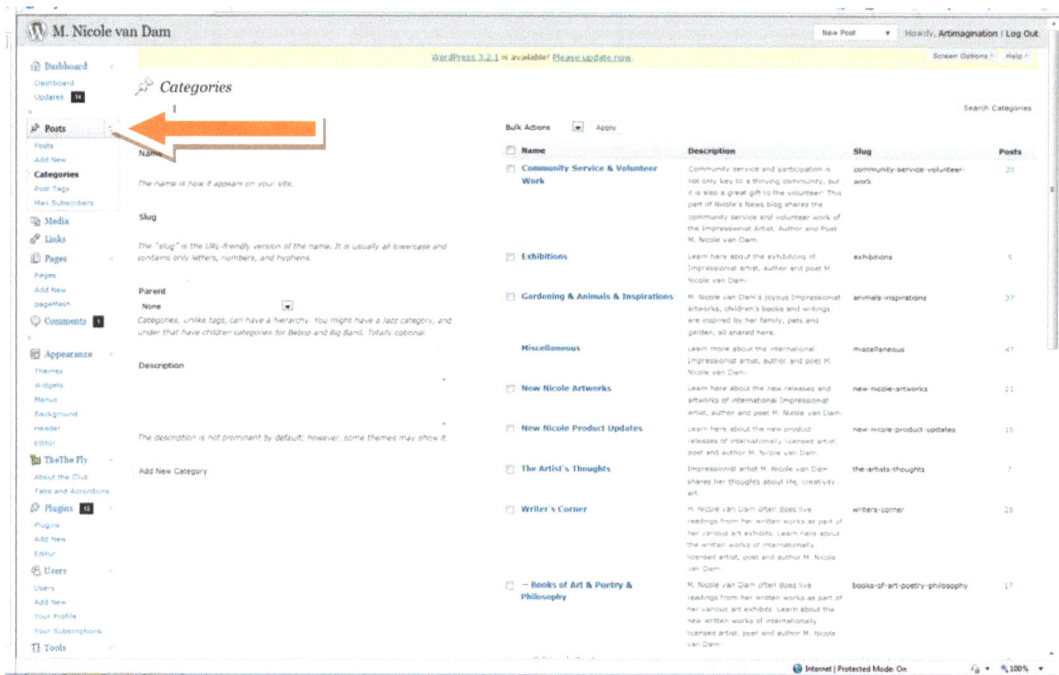

Step 15 - How to Create Additional Pages and How to Work with the Pages Widget

Pages are different than posts. Posts appear on a web page, and you can have more than one post per web page. Pages are actually the web pages of your site. If you have followed along this book, you will already have an e-commerce page to your site, created through the ecwid plugin, and you will have the default blog post that Wordpress automatically creates for you when you use the Wordpress software. In addition, you might wish to have an "About Us' page, or a "Careers" page, etc. This Section 15 overviews how you add more pages.

1. *Adding Pages:*

   To add pages, just click "Add New" under the "Pages" drop down menu as shown below.

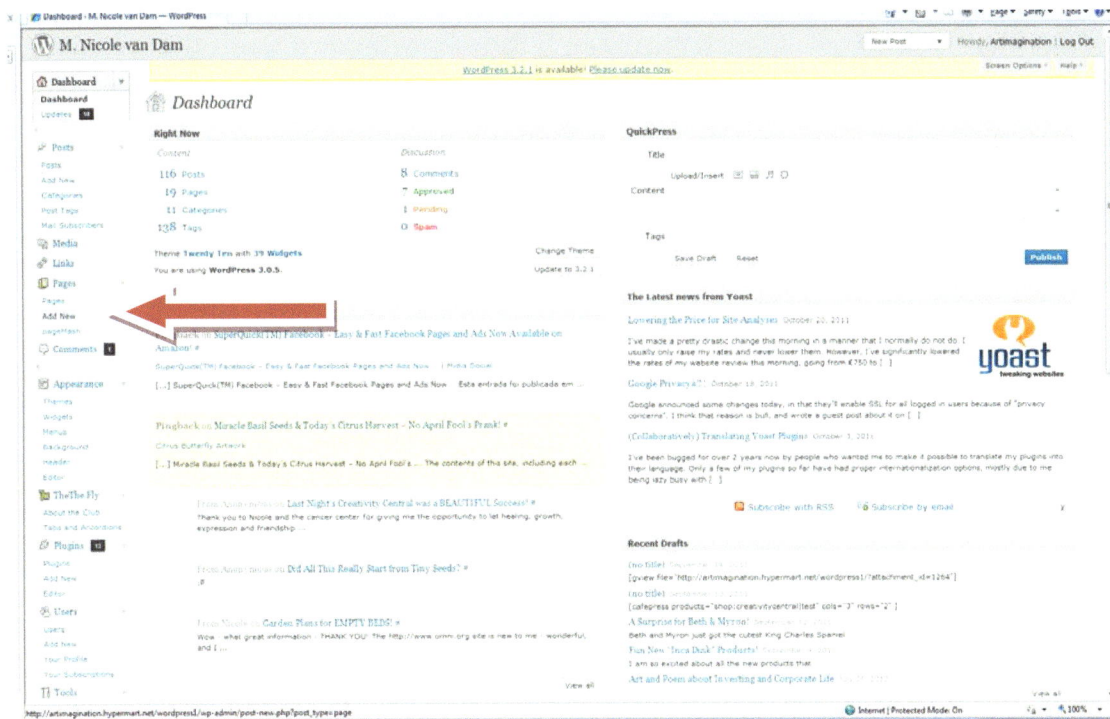

Clicking "Add New" under the Pages menu, as just shown, brings you to this page:

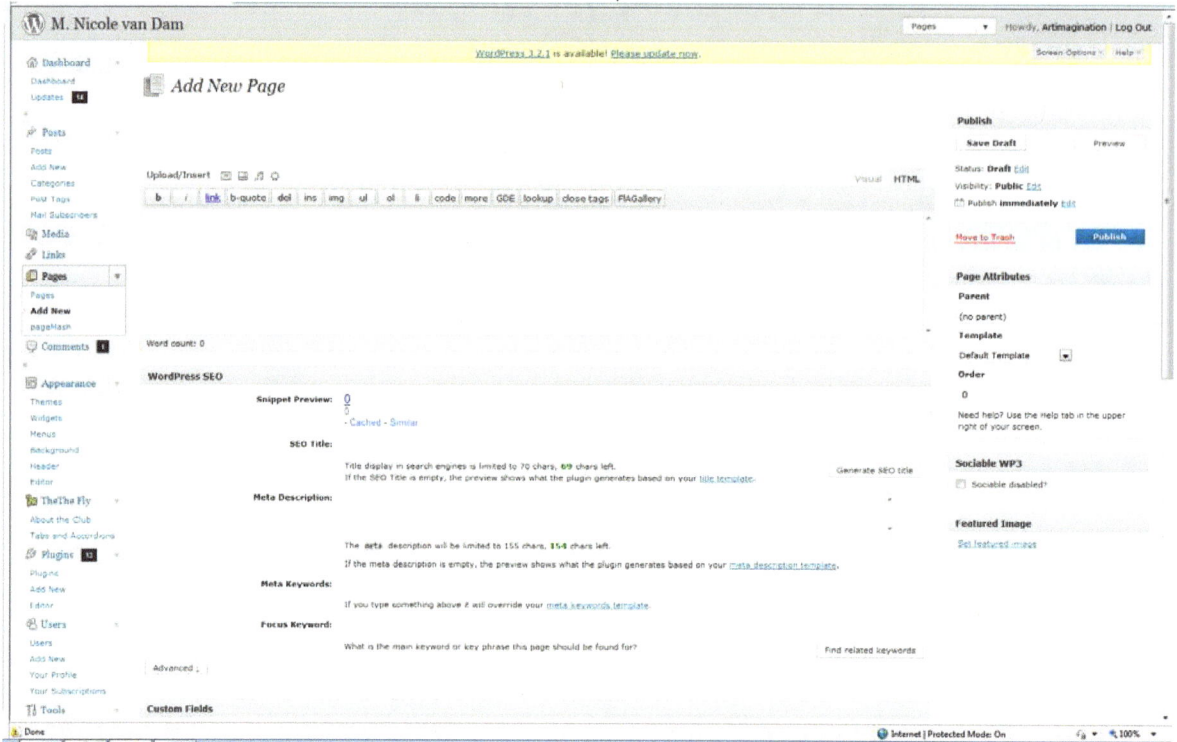

As shown below, in this Page workspace you can:
Type in the "Title" of this particular page of your website, as shown by the ▲

Type in the content of the page in the content box shown by the ⬠ *, including HTML (make sure the HTML tab is clicked at the upper right of this content box). You can find good free HTML code on the web to cut and paste here, including at free sites like quackit.com.*

Choose how the page fits into your "Page" widget hierarchy, by deciding which pre-existing page (if any) will be the parent page for this page. See "Page Attributes" marked by the to experiment with "parent" pages. See Also Section 2 for more info.

Preview or Publish your new page, from the "Publish" area, shown by the ⬤ *.*

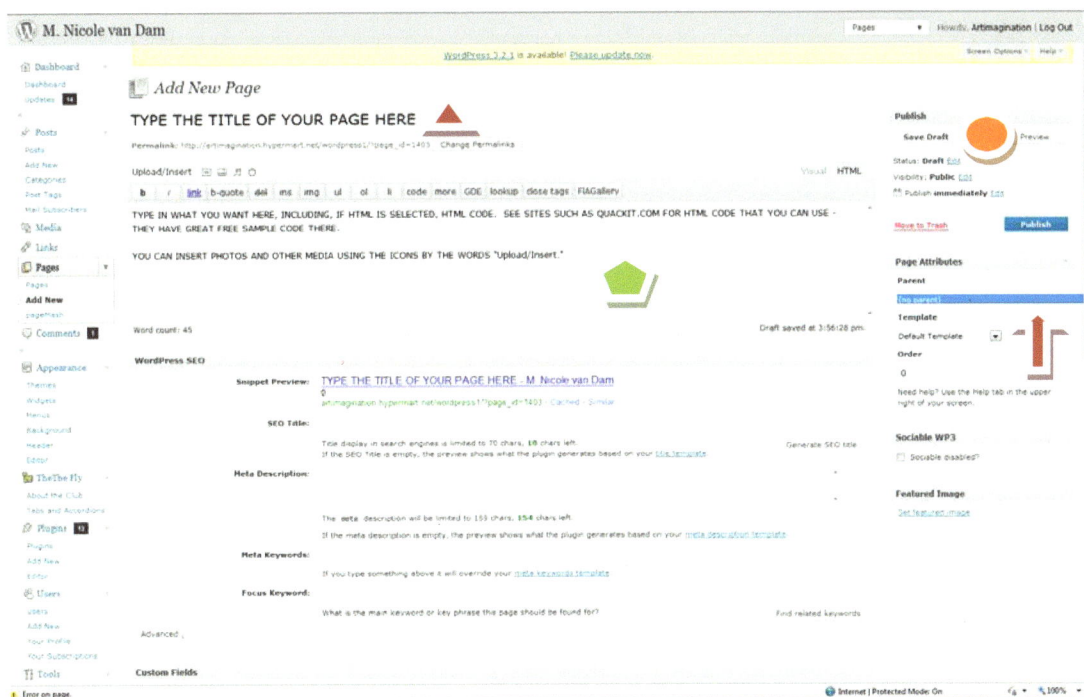

NOTE: If you choose to add the "Yoast SEO Plugin" as shown in the ADVANCED Plugins section, you can also do your search engine optimization from this page.

When you have successfully created a new page, it will show up on a list of pages, as shown below:

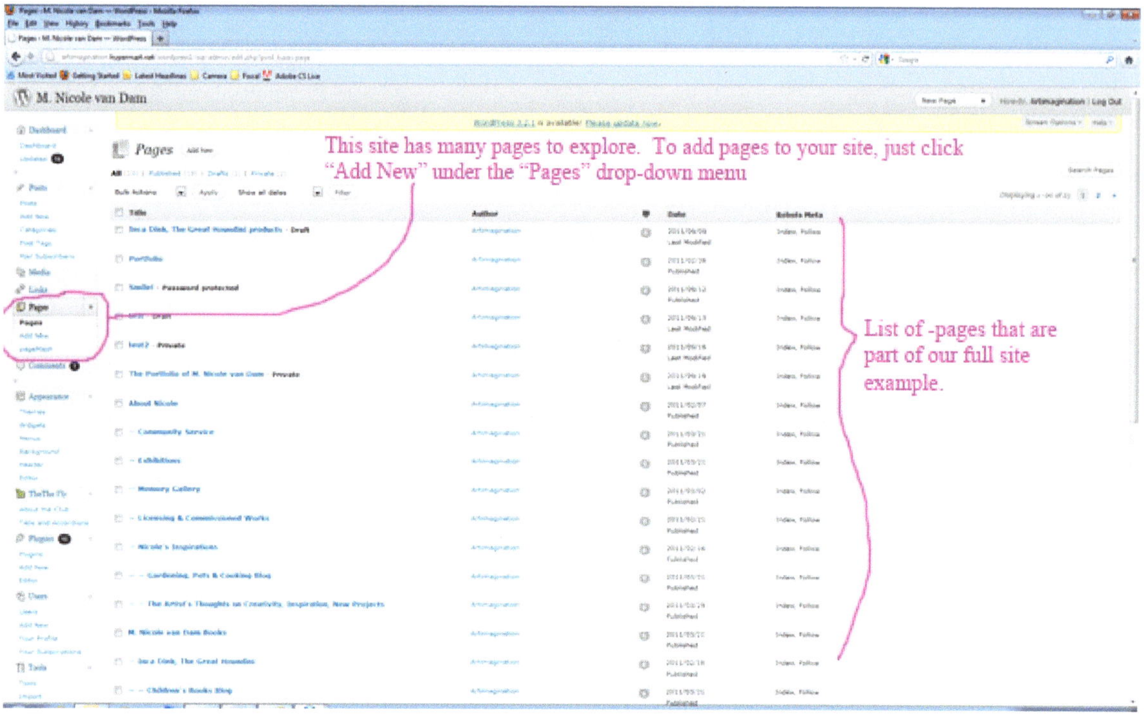

As shown below, if you roll your mouse over a page name on this list, a drop down menu appears that lets you choose to do one of several things, such as "Edit" or "Quick Edit."

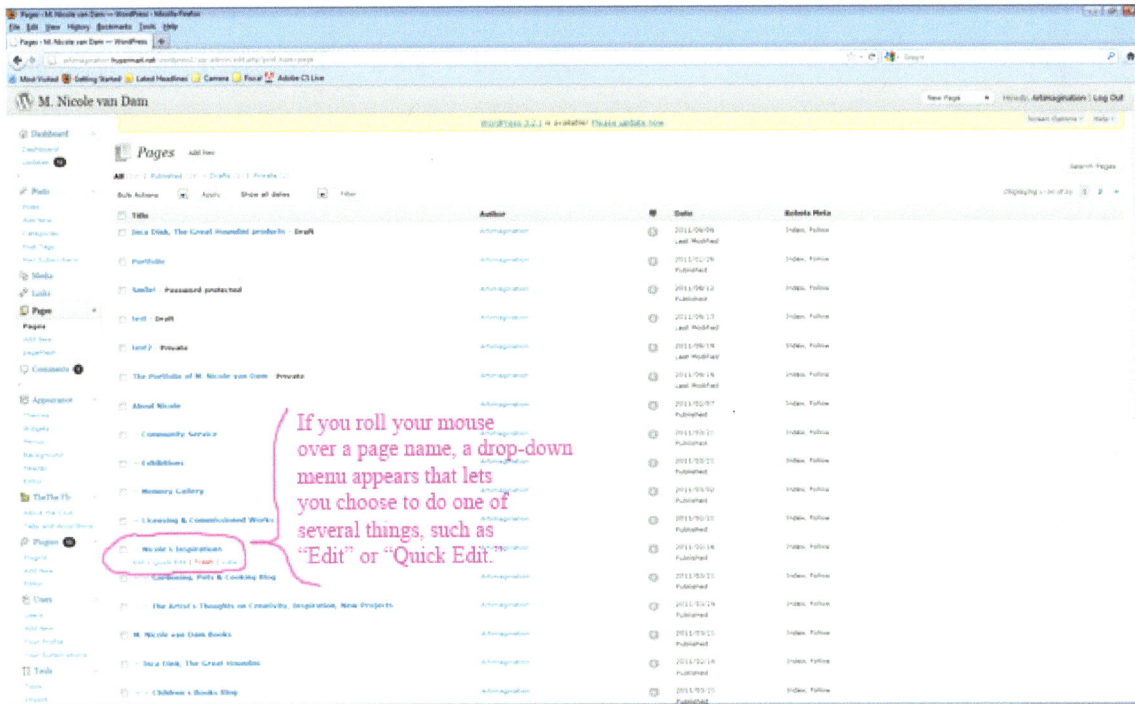

If you roll your mouse over a page name, a drop-down menu appears that lets you choose to do one of several things, such as "Edit" or "Quick Edit."

Choosing "Edit" lets you once again edit the page itself, as shown in the text input box below, marked with the <u>orange double-arrow</u>:

2. *More on the "Pages" Widget:* **Adding New Pages Changes the "Pages" Widget**:

   *If you choose "Quick Edit" instead of "Edit" then you change a page title **or select where in your page hierarchy this page should show up if you are using the "Pages" widget**:*

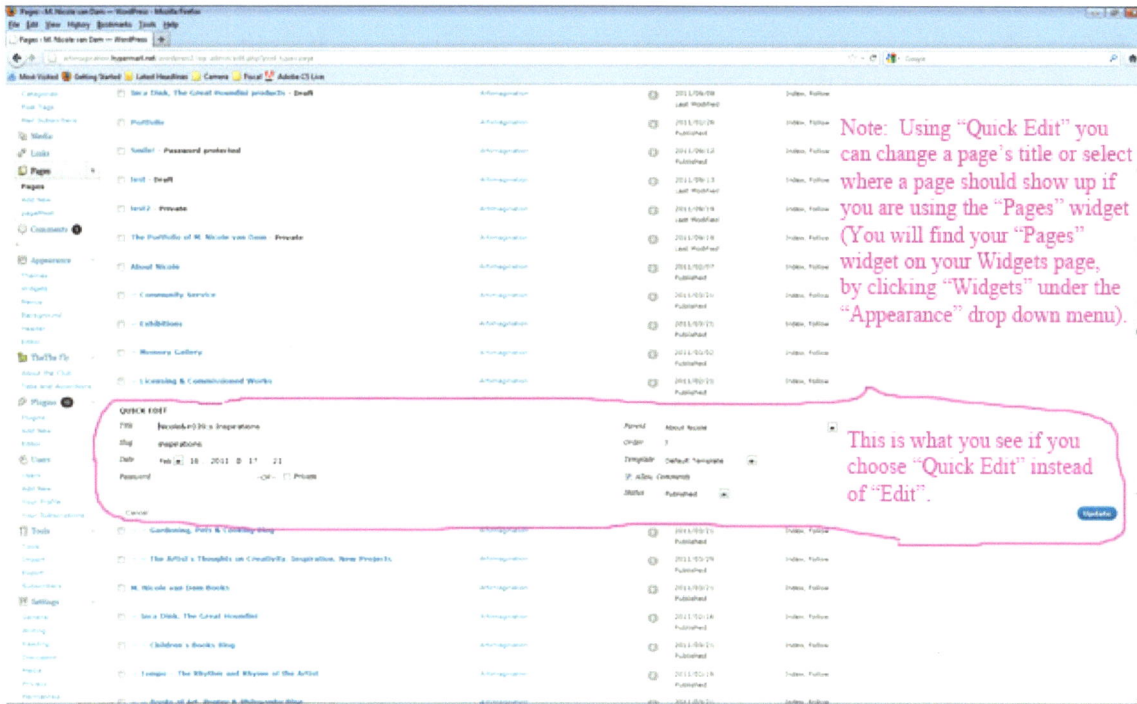

Note: Using "Quick Edit" you can change a page's title or select where a page should show up if you are using the "Pages" widget (You will find your "Pages" widget on your Widgets page, by clicking "Widgets" under the "Appearance" drop down menu).

This is what you see if you choose "Quick Edit" instead of "Edit".

Reminder: You will find the "Pages" widget on your "Widgets" workspace by clicking "Widgets" under the "Appearance" dropdown menu, as discussed in Part 2 of this book.

Below is a reminder showing where the "Pages" widget is in the "Widgets" workspace for this example:

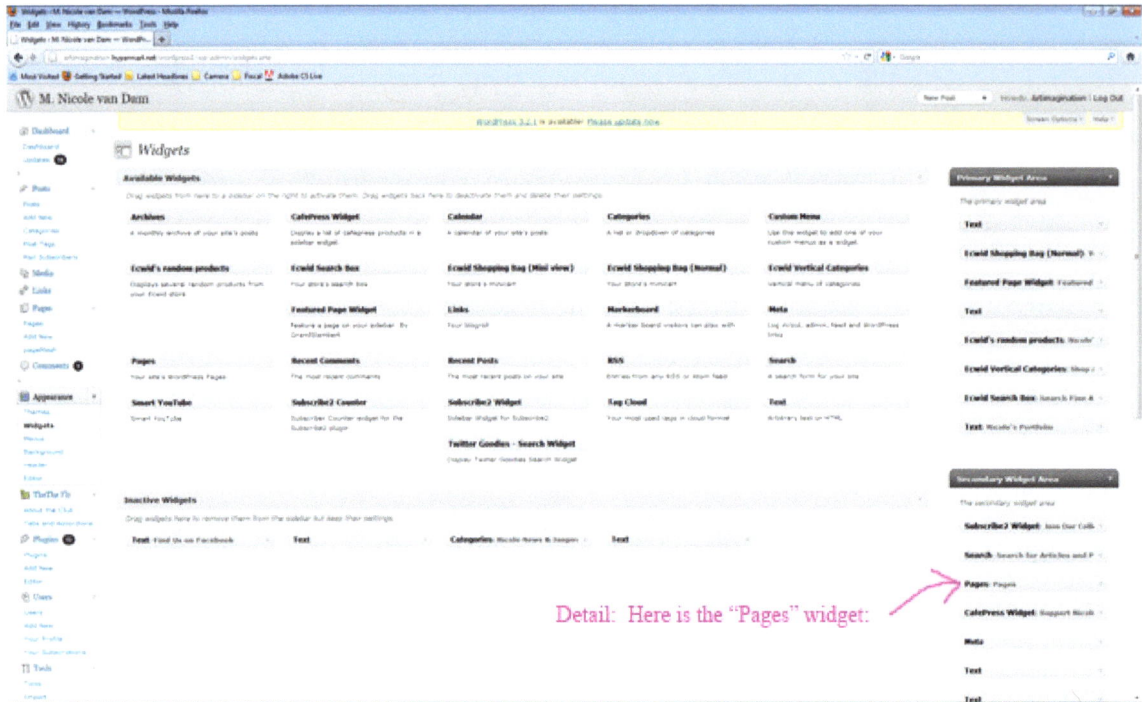

Detail: Here is the "Pages" widget:

PICTORAL SUMMARY: Whether you select the "Parent" page in the main Edit Pages workspace or via choosing the "Parent" page in "Quick Edit" as shown below:

-So choosing the "Parent" page in "Quick Edit" as shown here

What page you select as the "Parent" page for a particular page will make the following page hierarchy automatically show up on your website via your "Pages" widget-see below:

Makes this hierarchy of pages automaitcally show up on your website via your "Pages" widget

Step 16- Customizing Your Header Menu bar (along the top under the header image)

1. First thing is to understand that the page menu you see in the black bar below the header image (see the ▲ below) is DIFFERENT from the Pages hierarchy (shown in the prior illustration marked by the ⬤ that you see on your site when you use the "Pages" widget.

Customizing the Menu changes the menu choices that are directly under your header image:

Customized Menu choices means that you can choose which pages you want to show up here at the top menu.

In this Step we are going to discuss how to customize that black menu bar directly underneath the image header.

2. *Under the "Appearance" menu on the Dashboard, choose "Menus" as shown by the* ⬆ *below:*

3. *Customize your menu by checking the checkbox by each page you wish to add to the header menu, as shown by the* ⊗ *above;*
4. *Once you have checked the pages you wish to add to your header menu, click "Add to Menu" as shown by the* ▲ *above;*
5. *Now the pages you selected will show up on the custom menu shown by the* ⬇ *above.* **You can drag and drop your pages in the custom menu workspace to place your pages exactly in the order you wish to see in the header menu.**
6. *Remember to click "Save Menu" (see the* ▼ *in the upper right corner) to save your work!*

Following is the result of your creating a custom header menu – see the *below:*

Part 5 Advanced Design, Plugins and Widgets
Identifying and Using Key Plugins & Widgets

Here is what my site looks like as of this writing. I have in hot pink labeled the various elements of the site with the names of the widgets or process used to create this site. After the screen captures I will show you the "back end" so you can see which plugins and widgets I used to get there:

Step 17 - Identifying Key Plugins & Widgets on a Website

1. *The first step is to look at what a full website looks like. Following are screen captures of my website as of this writing. In pink I have notated what I used to create each element.*

The top portion of my website:

CUSTOM HEADER IMAGE: See the ⟶ *below; Creating this was discussed in Step 5.*

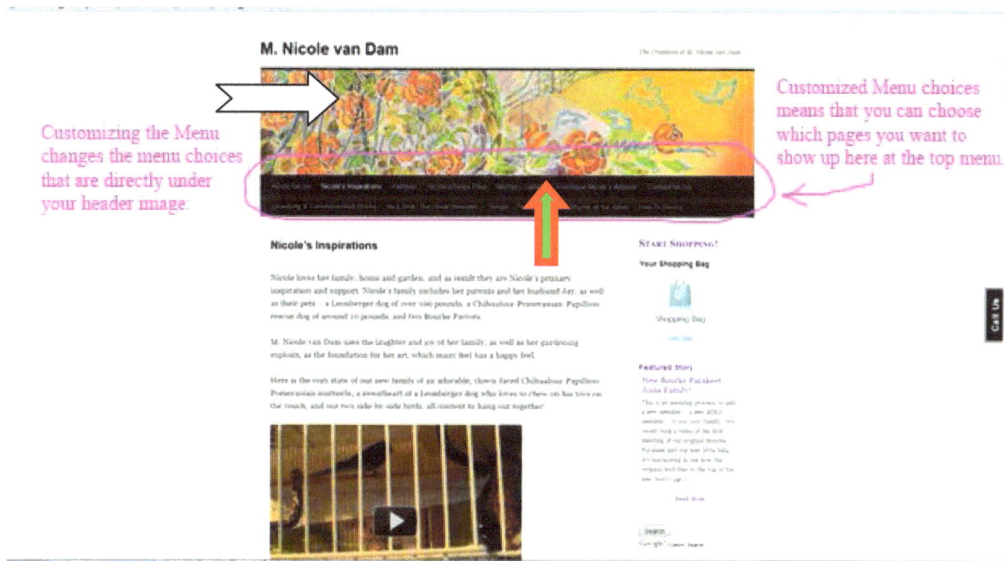

CUSTOM MENU: You will note by the ⬆ *above that I have many different pages in the custom header menu bar directly below the header. This customized header menu bar is created through customizing my menu choices as shown in Step 16 of this book.*

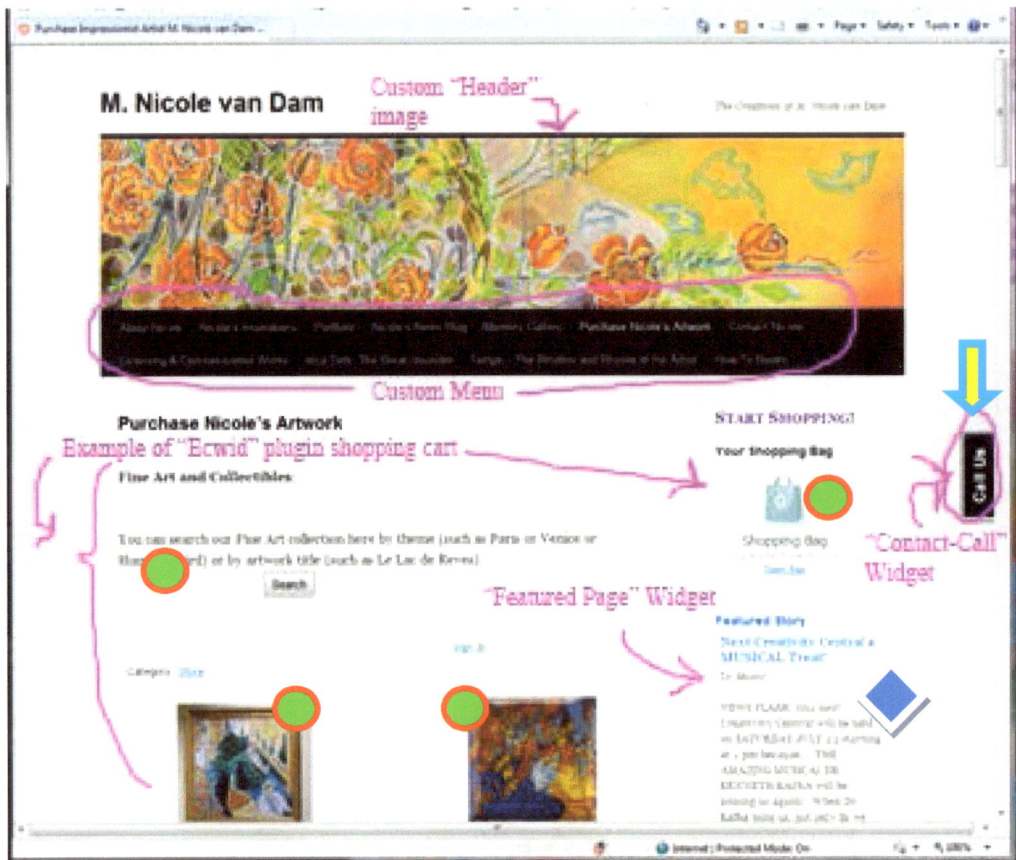

M. Nicole van Dam

Custom "Header" image

Custom Menu

Purchase Nicole's Artwork

Example of "Ecwid" plugin shopping cart

Fine Art and Collectibles

START SHOPPING!

Your Shopping Bag

Shopping Bag

"Contact-Call" Widget

"Featured Page" Widget

ECWID: Above by the ⬤ *symbols you can see the results of installing and implementing the Ecwid plugin shopping cart, as we went over in Part 3 of this book.*

"FEATURED PAGE": By the ◆ *you can also see the "Featured Page" widget, which randomly picks a page/blog post to highlight – this keeps your content looking fresh.*

"CONTACT-CALL" WIDGET: The ⬇ *above designates the "Contact-Call" is a free widget that lets users around the world call you –using Skype or a phone - for free! This free service also emails you when someone tries to reach you. Just search for "Contact-Call" when you are at the "Add New" plugins search box on the plugins page workspace.*

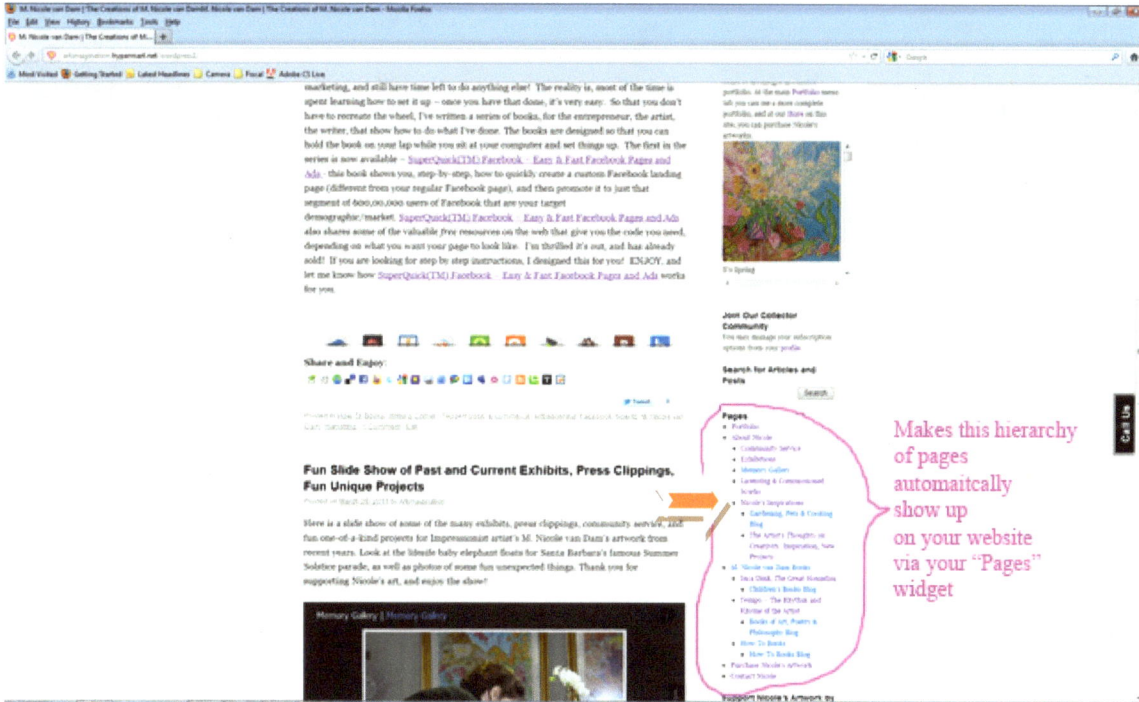

Annotation on image: Makes this hierarchy of pages automaitcally show up on your website via your "Pages" widget

"PAGES" WIDGET: As shown above by the ➤➤➤ and as discussed in depth in Part 4, the "Pages" widget lists the pages you add to your Wordpress site in whatever hierarchy you choose.

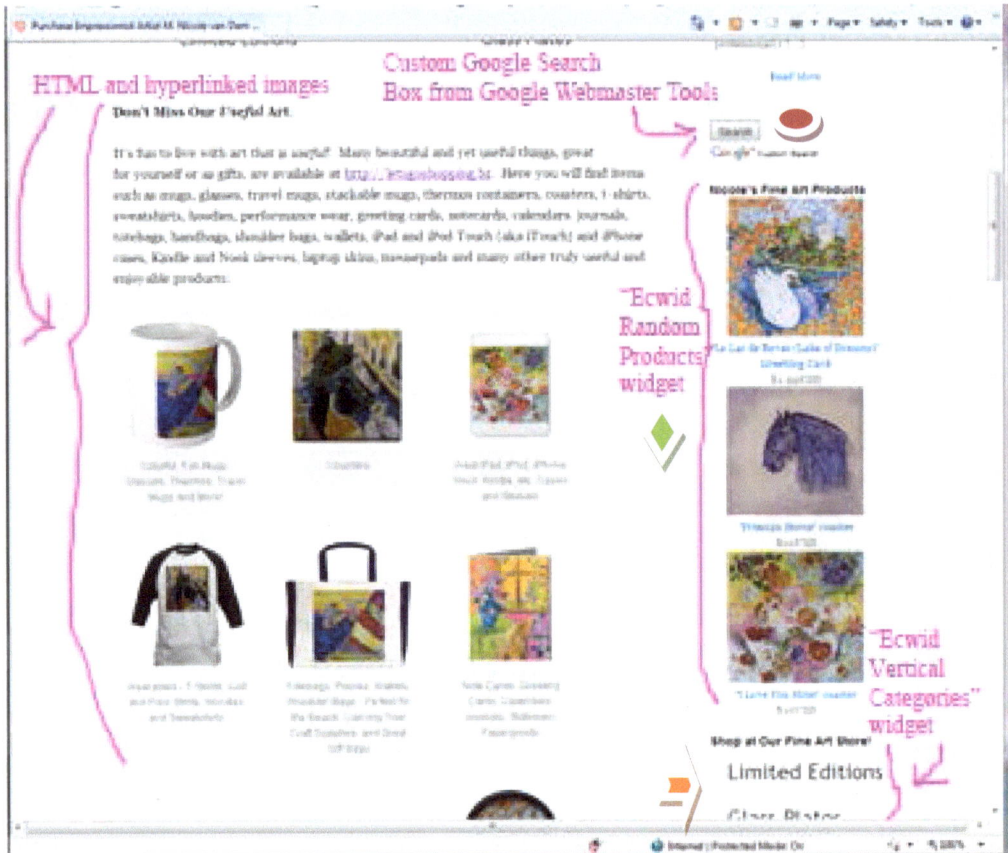

HTML PAGE: The left center portion of the above page was created as set forth in Step 15 using HTML and hyperlinked images. Free html code can be found on the web, such as at quackit.com

GOOGLE CUSTOM SEARCH: This is a nifty search engine where you customize the world to be searched, which you can obtain via Google's Webmaster tools on the Google website. See the ⬤ to help you find this element.

"ECWID RANDOM PRODUCTS" WIDGET: on the right side by the ◆ you will see a widget you can download as a plugin – just search for the "Ecwid Random Products" when you are at the "Add New" plugins search box on the plugins page workspace.

"ECWID VERTICAL CATEGORIES" WIDGET: This ▬ is an option that appears on your Widgets work space when you install the ecwid plugin as discussed in detail in Part 3.

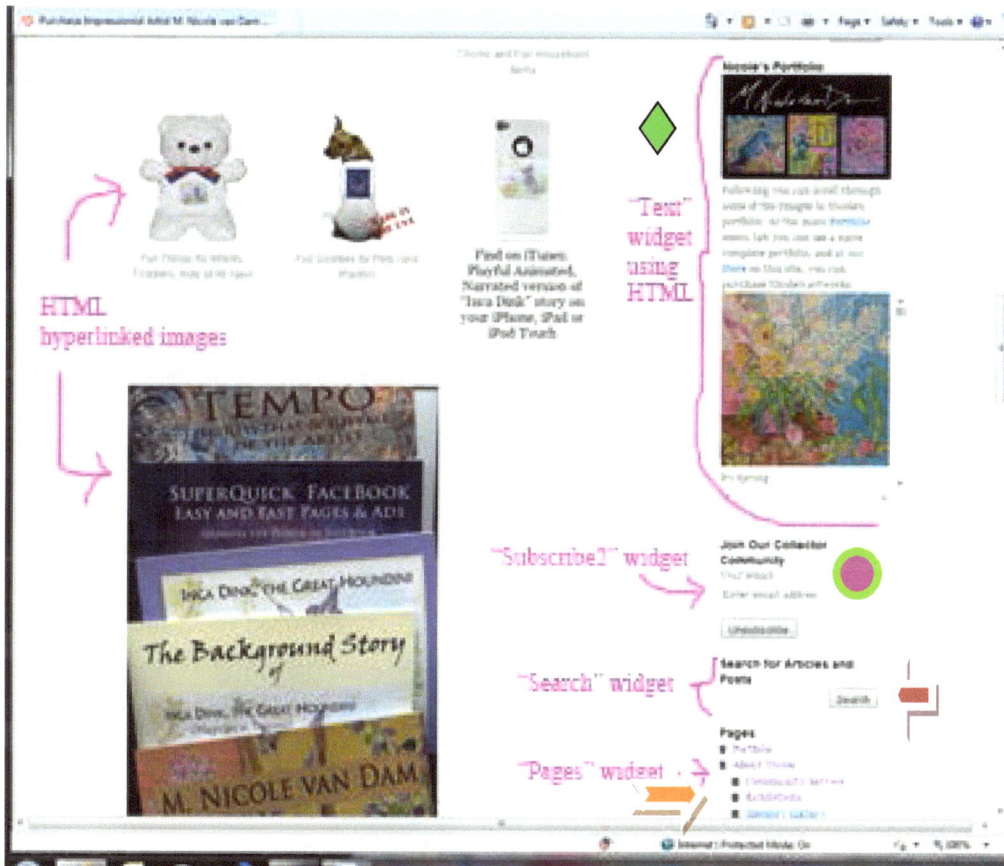

HTML PAGE: The left center portion of the above page was created as set forth in Step 15 using HTML and hyperlinked images. Free html code can be found on the web, such as at quackit.com

"TEXT" WIDGET: See ◆ *. The text widget at upper right was created using HTML and hyperlinked images. Free html code can be found on the web, such as at quackit.com*

"SUBSCRIBE2" WIDGET: See ⬤ *This can be downloaded as a plugin - just search for the "Subscribe2" when you are at the add new plugins search box on the plugins page workspace*

"SEARCH" WIDGET: See ▬ *This "Search" widget automatically comes standard with Wordpress. This "Search" widget is DIFFERENT from the Google Custom Search that you also see on this site, discussed elsewhere in this section. I use both!*

"PAGES" WIDGET: As shown in the preceding illustration and below, in each case marked by the *and as discussed in depth in Part 4, the "Pages" widget lists the pages you add to your Wordpress site in whatever hierarchy you choose.*

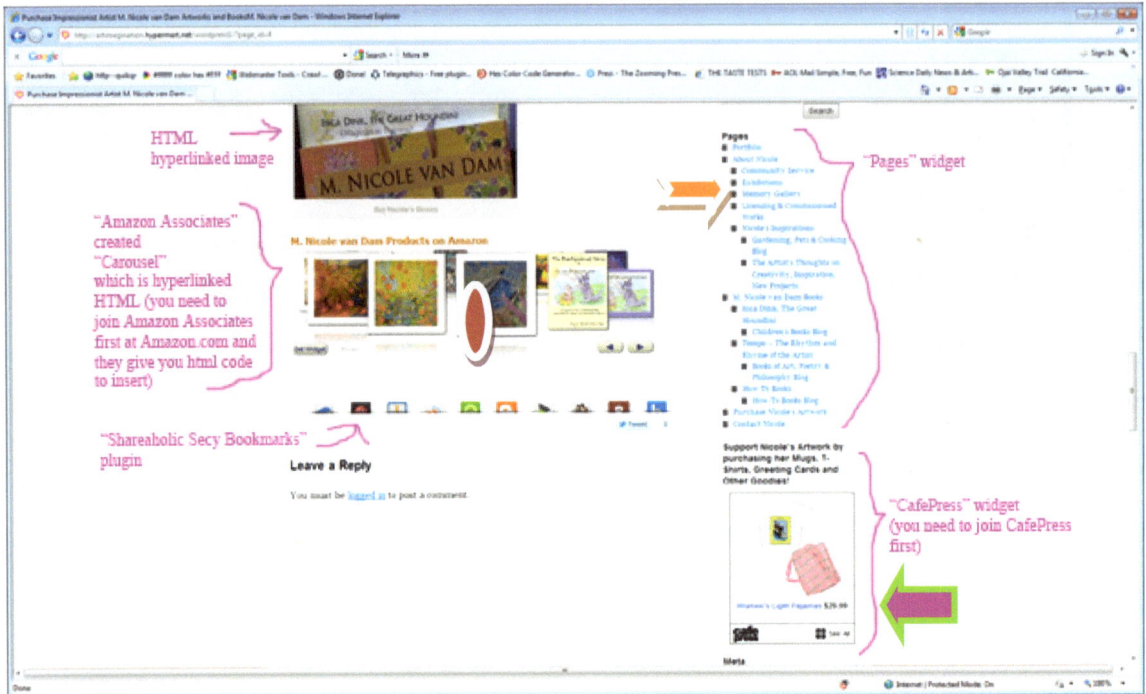

HTML PAGE: The upper left portion of the above page was created as set forth in Step 15 using HTML and hyperlinked images. Free html code can be found on the web, such as at quackit.com

AMAZON ASSOCIATES CAROUSEL: This *is a nifty rotating carousel of products for sale on Amazon, where you choose the products to be shown on the carousel. You obtain the html code for this carousel via your Amazon Associates account at Amazon.com.*

"PAGES" WIDGET: As shown above and as discussed in depth in Part 4, the "Pages" widget lists the pages you add to your Wordpress site in whatever hierarchy you choose. See the *symbol above.*

"CAFEPRESS" WIDGET: See *This widget lets you highlight items for sale on your Cafepress.com website – In other words, you need a cafepress.com account first.*

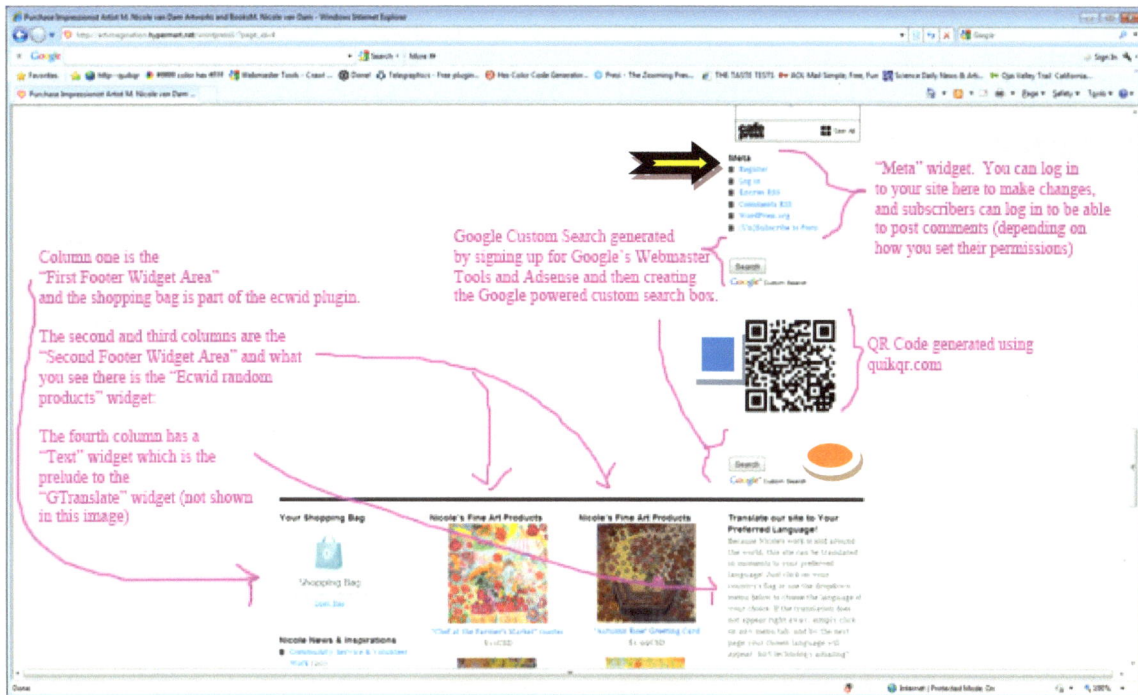

"META" WIDGET: In the upper right corner above you will see the Meta widget. The Meta widget automatically appears as one of your available widgets on your Widgets page workspace area. Use this widget so that users of your site (and you) can easily register (user registration helps you build a customer and newsletter email database) and log in to your site. The Meta widget is also critical when you set your Dashboard Settings preferences so that only registered users can write comments to your blog posts. See ➤ above.

QR CODE: The QR CODE was created for free using quikqr.com and inserted into the widget area using the "Text" widget. As you might recall from prior sections of this book – the "Text" widget allows you to insert regular text OR html code (including hyperlinked images). See ▮

GOOGLE CUSTOM SEARCH: This is a nifty search engine where you customize the world to be searched, which you can obtain via Google's Webmaster tools on the Google website. See ⬭

The next page continues the discussion on this screen capture.

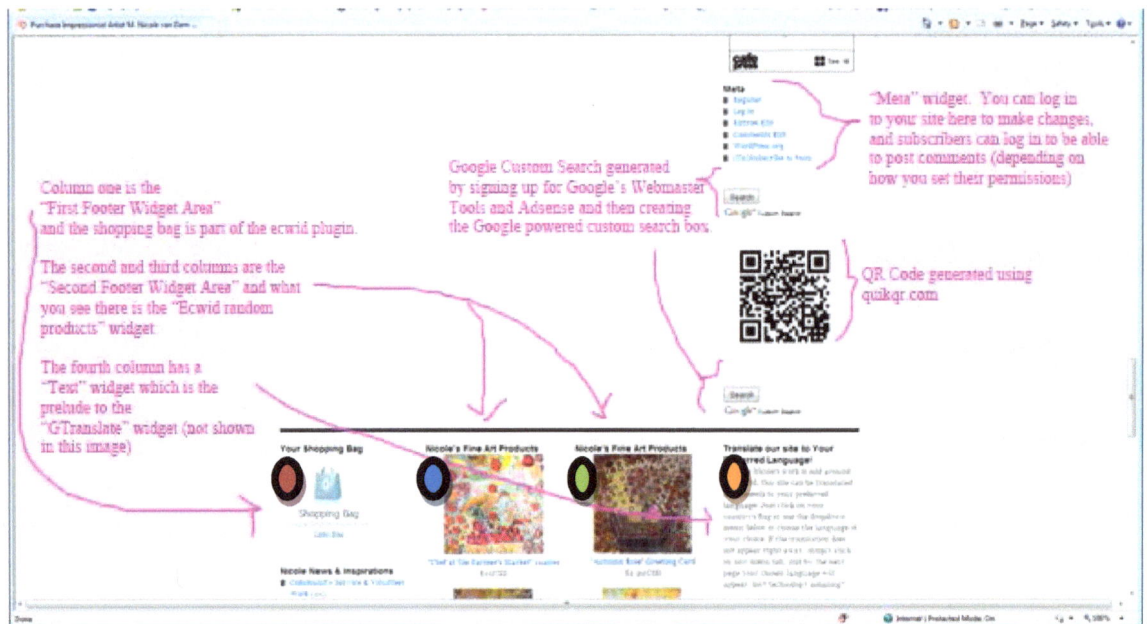

Column one is the
"First Footer Widget Area"
and the shopping bag is part of the ecwid plugin.

The second and third columns are the
"Second Footer Widget Area" and what
you see there is the "Ecwid random
products" widget.

The fourth column has a
"Text" widget which is the
prelude to the
"GTranslate" widget (not shown
in this image)

Google Custom Search generated
by signing up for Google's Webmaster
Tools and Adsense and then creating
the Google powered custom search box.

"Meta" widget. You can log in
to your site here to make changes,
and subscribers can log in to be able
to post comments (depending on
how you set their permissions)

QR Code generated using
quikqr.com

Underneath the solid black line, along the bottom, you can see the four "Footer Widget Areas" as follows:

- First Footer Widget Area (furthest left)(See ⬤): The shopping bag is part of the Ecwid e-commerce plug in we installed in Part 3 of this book.

- Second ⬤ and Third Footer ⬤ Widget Areas: Both of these footer areas respectively have the "Ecwid Random Products" widget – this is a widget you can download as a plugin – just search for the "Ecwid Random Products" when you are at the "Add New" plugins search box on the plugins page workspace.

- Fourth Footer Widget Area (the furthest right column – see ⬤): This is the introductory paragraph (created using the "Text" widget) which serves as the prelude for the "GTranslate" plugin which automatically translates your site into one of dozens of languages upon a user's request. The actual results of the GTranslate plugin are shown on the next screen capture.

102

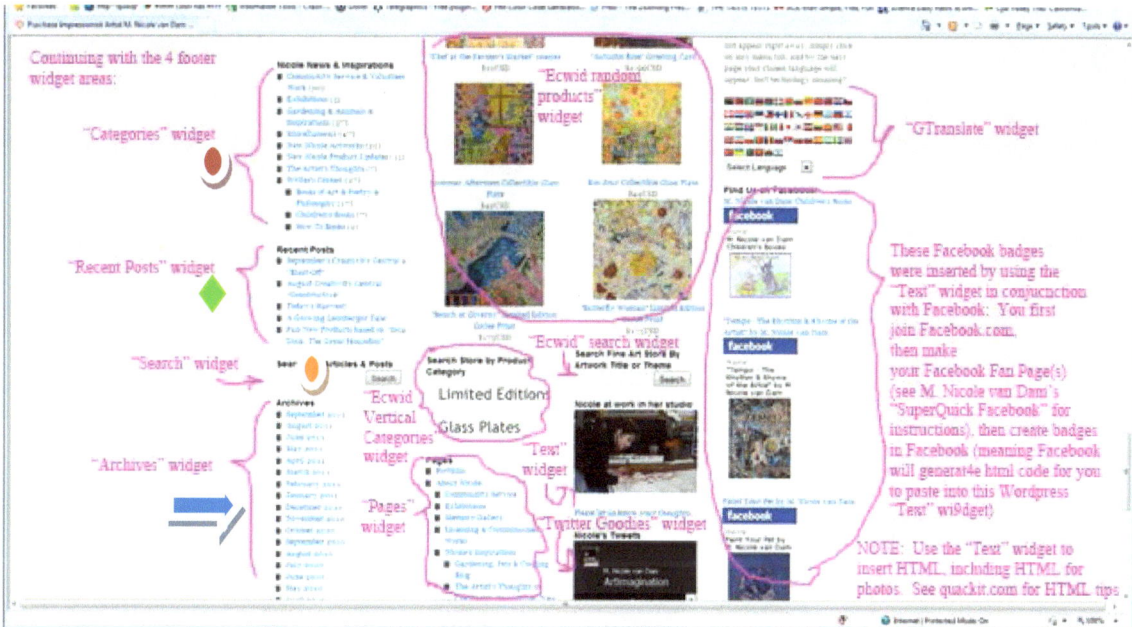

The above screen capture shows the Four Footer Widget Areas, scrolling further down.

FIRST FOOTER WIDGET AREA   :

- *"CATEGORIES" WIDGET: See ● This widget lists all the categories you have created for your posts. The "Categories" widget automatically appears as one of your available widgets on your Widgets page workspace area. As a reminder, creating categories for your blog posts was discussed in detail in Part 4 of this book.*
- *"RECENT POSTS" WIDGET: See ◆ This widget lists your most recent blog posts. The "Recent Posts" widget automatically appears as one of your available widgets on your Widgets page workspace area. As a reminder, creating blog posts was discussed in detail in Part 4 of this book.*
- *"SEARCH" WIDGET: See ● "Search" widget automatically comes standard with Wordpress. This "Search" widget is DIFFERENT from the Google Custom Search that you also see on this site, discussed elsewhere in this section. I use both!*
- *"ARCHIVES" WIDGET: See ➡ This widget gives your users access to the archives of your blog posts. The "Archives" widget automatically appears as one of your available widgets on your Widgets page workspace area. As a reminder, creating blog posts was discussed in detail in Part 4 of this book. Wordpress automatically creates archives of your blog posts based on the preferences you choose in the Settings of your Wordpress Dashboard.*

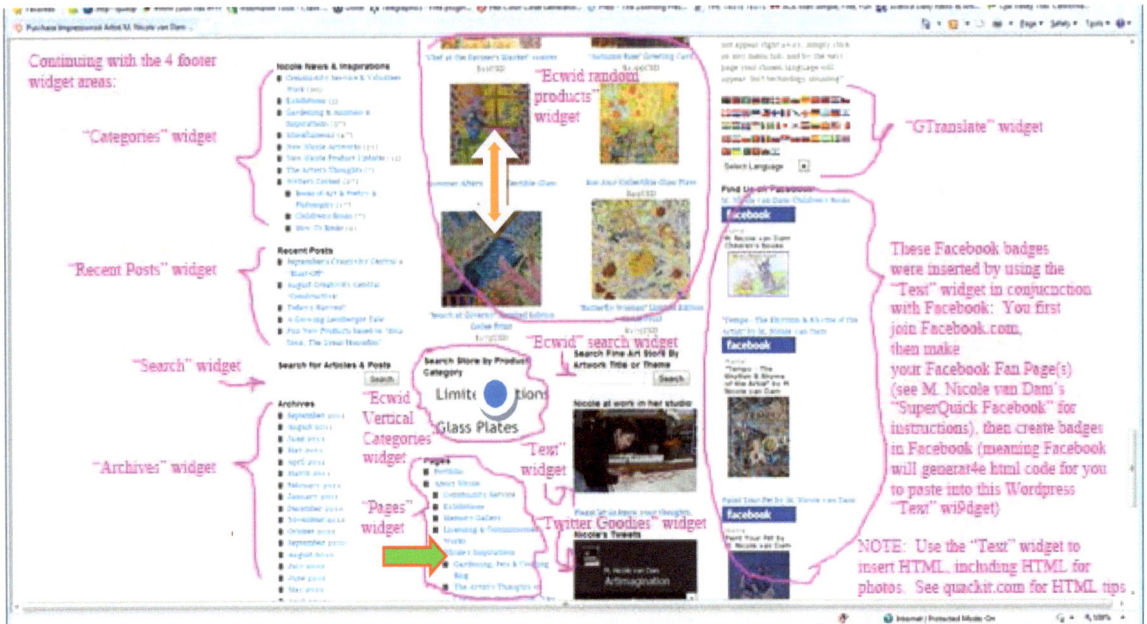

The above screen capture shows the Four Footer Widget Areas, scrolling further down.

SECOND FOOTER WIDGET AREA:

- "ECWID RANDOM PRODUCTS" WIDGET: See 🔼 this is a widget you can download as a plugin – just search for the "Ecwid Random Products" when you are at the "Add New" plugins search box on the plugins page workspace.

- "ECWID VERTICAL CATEGORIES" WIDGET: See 🔵 This is an option that appears on your Widgets work space when you install the ecwid plugin as discussed in detail in Part 3.

- "PAGES" WIDGET: As shown above and as discussed in depth in Part 4, the "Pages" widget lists the pages you add to your Wordpress site in whatever hierarchy you choose. See ➡️ in the screen capture above.

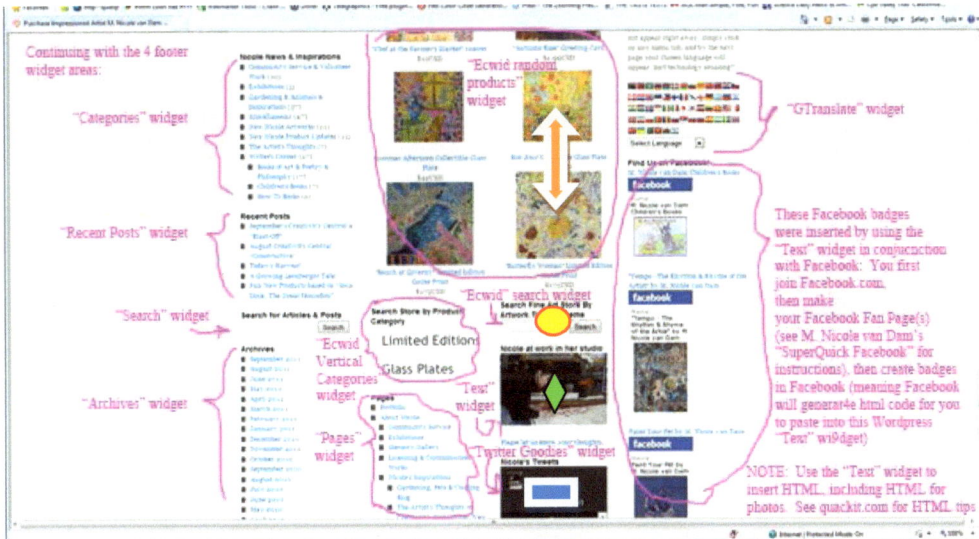

The above screen capture shows the Four Footer Widget Areas, scrolling further down.

THIRD FOOTER WIDGET AREA:

- *"ECWID RANDOM PRODUCTS" WIDGET: See ↓ this is a widget you can download as a plugin – just search for the "Ecwid Random Products" when you are at the "Add New" plugins search box on the plugins page workspace.*

- *"ECWID SEARCH" WIDGET: See ◯ This is an option that appears on your Widgets work space when you install the ecwid plugin as discussed in detail in Part 3. ECWID SEARCH only searches your ECWID store products, and it is therefore different from the regular "SEARCH WIDGET" which searches your whole blog, and also different from "Google Custom Search" which you set up using Google Webmaster Tools (Google Custom Search searches a larger universe than either of the other two search options).*

- *"TEXT" WIDGET: See ◆ The text widget at upper right was created using HTML and hyperlinked images. Free html code can be found on the web, such as at quackit.com*

- *"TWITTER GOODIES" WIDGET: See ▬ This widget will insert your Twitter tweets (so you need to set up a Twitter account and tweet to use this). To install widget just search for "Twitter Goodies" when you are at the "Add New" plugins search box on the plugins page workspace.*

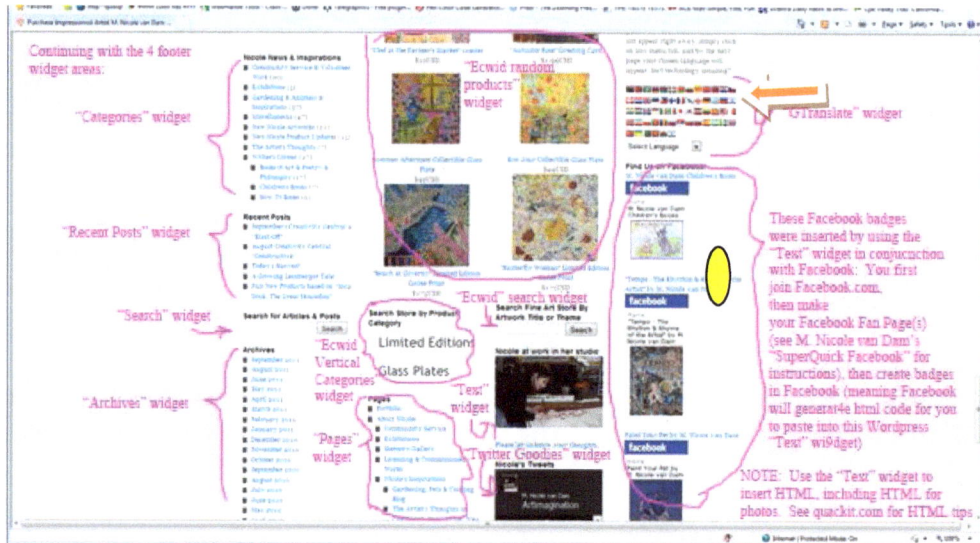

The above screen capture shows the Four Footer Widget Areas, scrolling further down.

FOURTH FOOTER WIDGET AREA:

- *"GTRANSLATE" WIDGET: See* ⬅ *The "GTranslate" widget automatically translates your site into one of dozens of languages upon a user's request.   To install widget just search for "Gtranslate" when you are at the "Add New" plugins search box on the plugins page workspace.*

- *FACEBOOK BADGES: See* ⬭ *If you have a Facebook account you can create Facebook badge code while on the Facebook website, and then copy that code and paste it into your Wordpress widget area using the "Text" widget.*

*NOTE: **It is a good idea to use the "Text" widget to include some kind of Intellectual Property notice in a Footer Widget Area, to protect your intellectual property. See your attorney for the best wording for your site.***

So now that we have identified all these widgets visually and by name, what does our widget workspace look like for all these widgets?

As discussed more fully in Step 6 of this book, by clicking on "Widgets" in the "Appearance" dropdown menu (see ⬅ *below), you will get to the Widgets workspace, where you can choose to see all the active widgets for your site. Below you can see screen captures of the Widgets workspace that generated my site:*

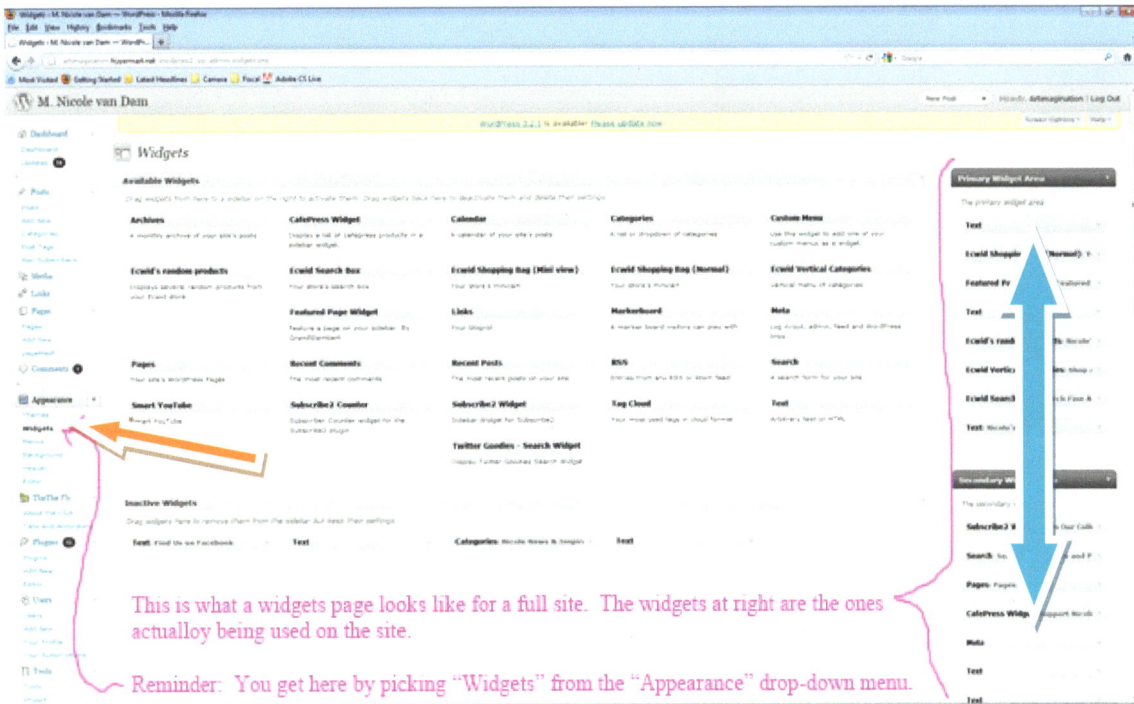

This is what a widgets page looks like for a full site. The widgets at right are the ones actualloy being used on the site.

Reminder: You get here by picking "Widgets" from the "Appearance" drop-down menu.

Remember from Step 6 of this Book that the "Active" Widgets are the widgets that appear in the right-most column of this Workspace, designated by the symbol in the above and following screen captures of the widget workspace.

The list of active widgets continues from the prior page:

-and the list of used widgets goes on!

Note 1: Wordpress divides
the used widgets into "Widget Areas" so that you can place the
widgets more easily where you want them.

Note 2: Where the "Widget Areas" will be on your site will
depend on which "Theme" you chose under the "Appearance" menu.
Having widgets on the right side and bottom is part of the Theme
we chose. Other Themes might have widgets on the top or left side, etc.

-and the list of active widgets continues even further:

and even more widgets are being used!

-and more active widgets:

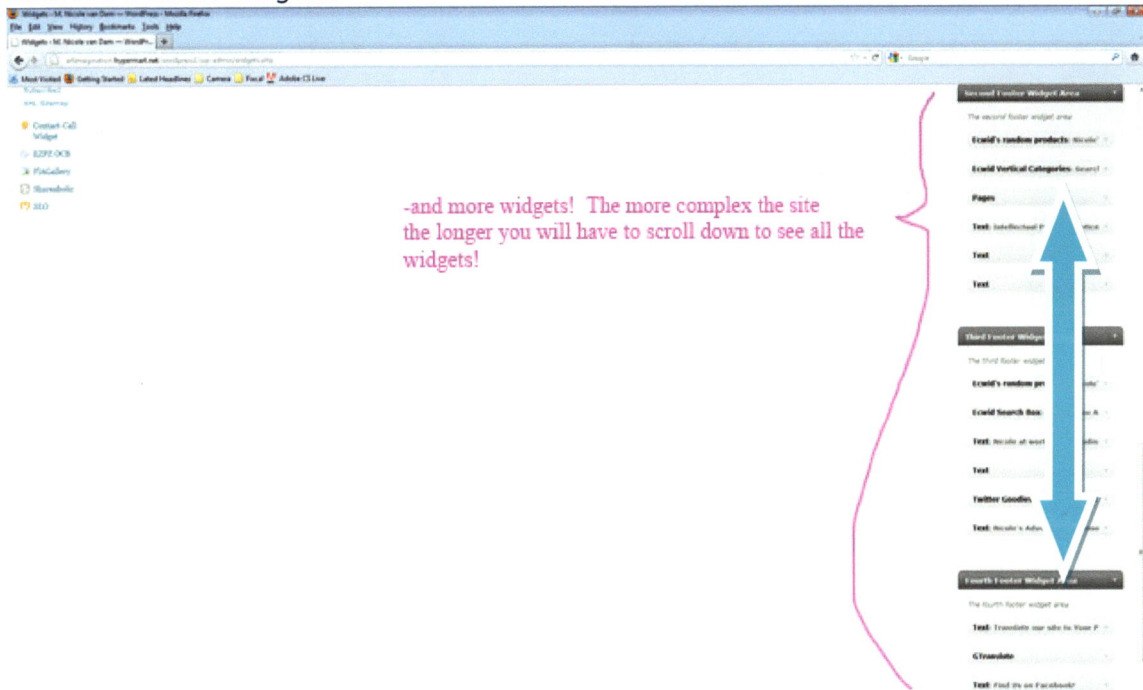

-and more widgets! The more complex the site the longer you will have to scroll down to see all the widgets!

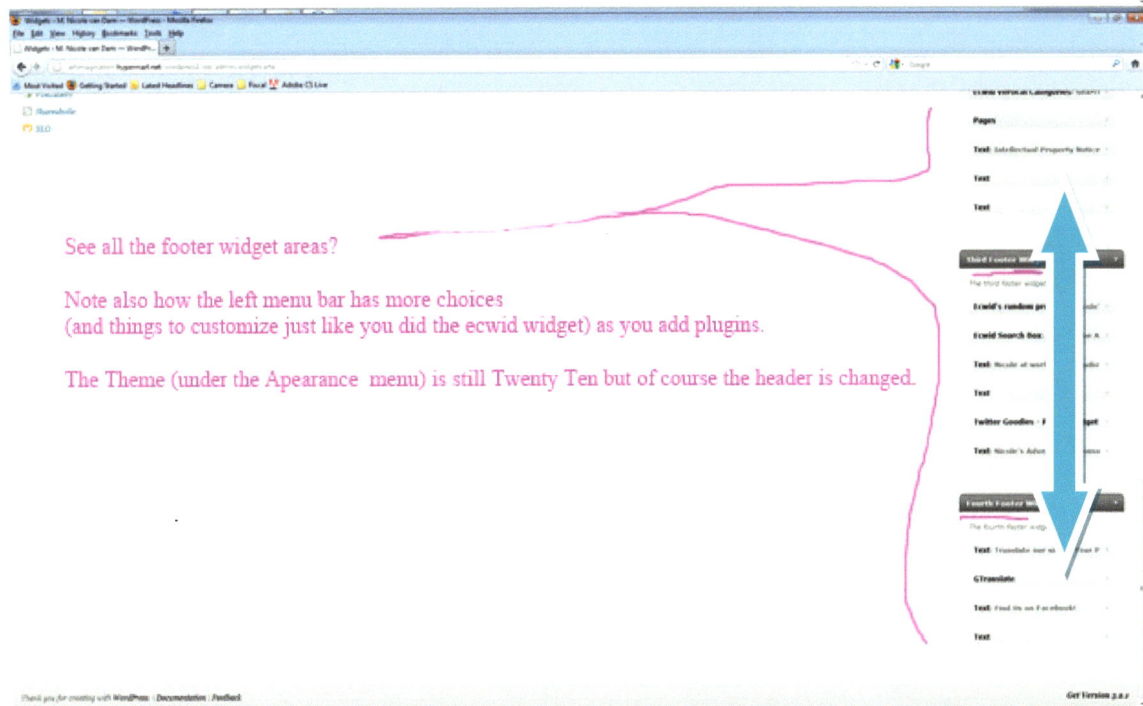

See all the footer widget areas?

Note also how the left menu bar has more choices
(and things to customize just like you did the ecwid widget) as you add plugins.

The Theme (under the Apearance menu) is still Twenty Ten but of course the header is changed.

Step 18 – Identifying Behind-the-Scenes Plugins & Widgets, including Backing Up Your Site, Search Engine Optimization, Smart Phone Capability & More!

1. By clicking on the Plugins menu (see ⬋ below), you will get to the Plugins workspace, where you can choose to see all the active plugins for your site. Below you can see a screen capture of the active Plugins that generated my site:

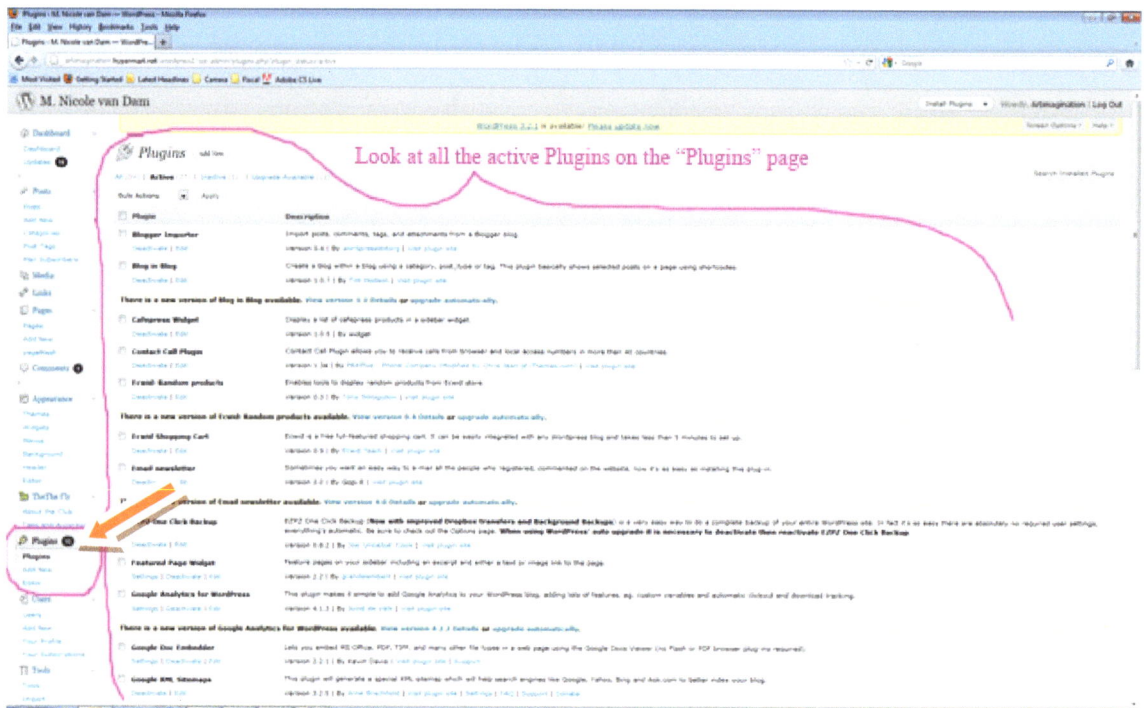

(screen captures of active plugins continued on next page)

-and the list of active "Plugins" goes on!

-and the list of active "plugins" goes on some more!

This doesn't mean each plugin used on every page. You can pick and choose where to use a plugin.

2. *The following Wordpress Plugins are noteworthy and useful, but these plugins generally aren't easily apparent from looking at a Wordpress site as a user. I included these plugins in this book so that you would know about them – they might be useful to you also!*

- *Blog-in-Blog plugin – In the event you wish to have **more than one blog page**, then this plugin will help you accomplish that, and will also help you manage which posts show up in which blog page.*

- *EZPZ One ClickBackup – it is important that you backup your site so in case something happens (a virus, hacker, host/server problem, whatever), then you can recreate what you have already done (in terms of pages AND posts) as easily as possible. The EZPZ One Click Backup plugin was created to help you do **regular scheduled backups**.*

- *FlAGallery plugin – helps you **manage your images as galleries and utilize slideshows** in your posts AND pages.*

- *Google Analytics (specifically for Wordpress Configuration) – helps you **implement Google Analytics** into your Wordpress site.*

- *pageMash – provides another workspace that for some might make it visually more intuitive to **manage your pages** in the Wordpress Dashboard.*

- *Shareaholic (SexyBookmarks) Plugin – enables users to easily **share your web content on more than 80 social networks**, and to choose how that sharing feature looks.*

- *TheTheFly Plugin – helps you **create tabs and accordions/sliders** on your pages.*

- *Wufoo Shortcode Plugin (use to **incorporate your Wufoo survey forms** – this is only useful if you have a Wufoo account)*

- *WPtouch – this Wordpress plugin will help your site **work with Smart Phones**. WPtouch currently lists the following as user agents for devices*

112

that WPtouch supports: Android, CUPCAKE, Googlebot-Mobile, bada, blackberry 9800, blackberry9500, blackberry9520, dream, iPhone, iPod, incognito, s8000, webOS, and webmate

- *Yoast SEO – this will help you preform "**Search Engine Optimization**" on your individual site pages AND your blog posts, as you create them.   In other words, the act of "Search Engine Optimization" (whether through this Yoast SEO plugin or otherwise) will help search engines find relevant portions of your site more easily. How the Yoast SEO changes the workspace where you edit Pages is shown below (see the <u>orange arrow</u> below):*

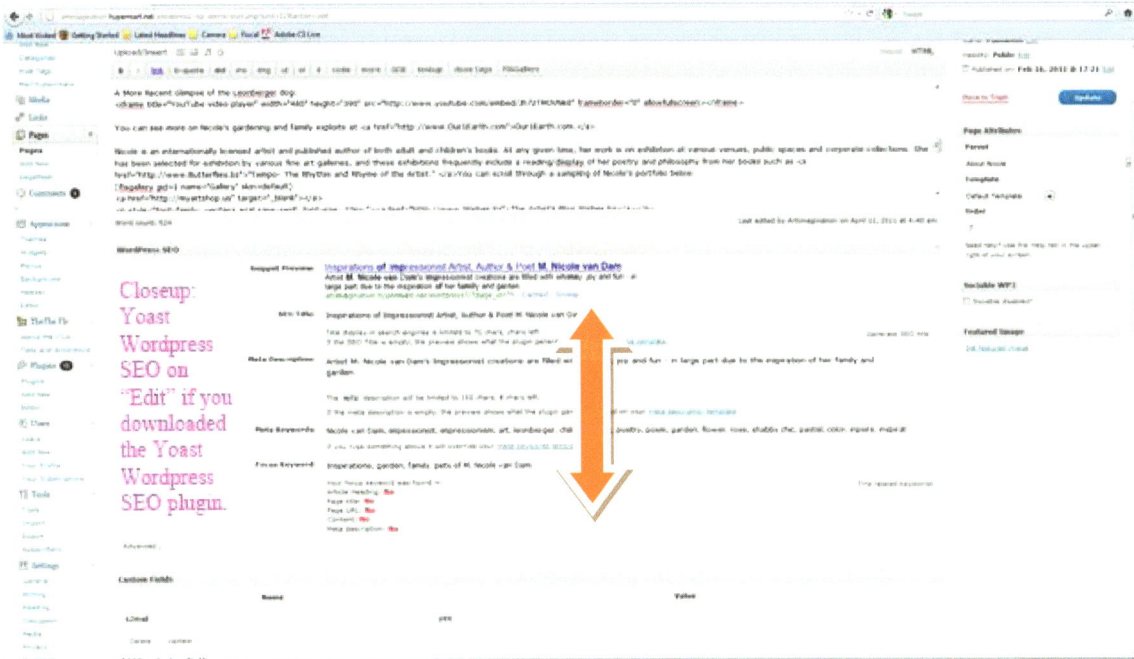

APPENDIX

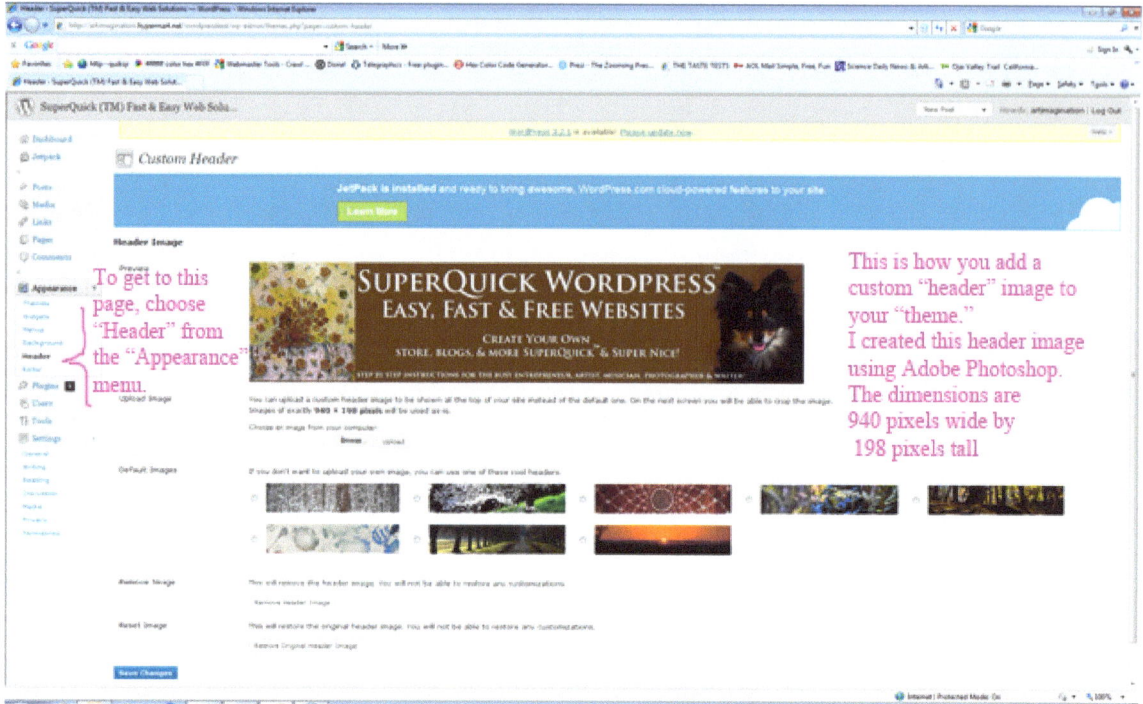

Illustrated detail on how to size an image using Adobe *Photoshop:*

As shown below, in Adobe Photoshop, simply click the "Image" menu item, which then gives you the drop down menu shown below. From this drop-down menu, choose "Image Size"

Choosing "Image Size" from the drop down menu, as shown above, brings you to the pop-up menu shown below, where you can change the size of your image, and you can choose to work in pixels or inches.

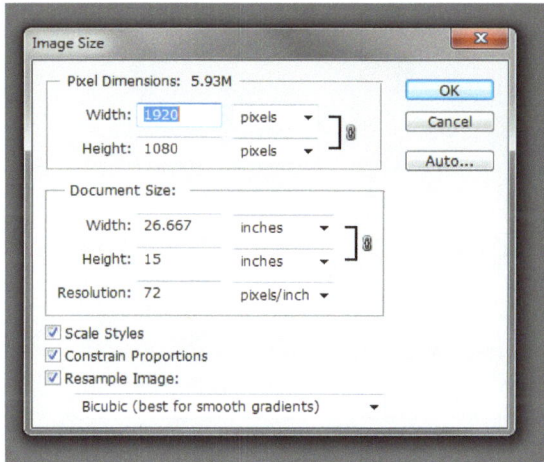

 72 dpi is a fine resolution for the web. If you click the check box for "Constrain Proportions" then the relative dimensions of your original image will stay the same; if that box is not clicked, then your image will be stretched to fit any new dimensions you choose. If I have to design to a particular size, such as 940x198 pixels for the Wordpress header, I either use an image that by itself lends itself to those dimensions or I use images with text to make up the difference in width; in other words, I would rather not stretch a single squarish image that far to be so much wider than tall unless I wanted a very abstract art look.

Thoughts to Ponder & Recommendations:

I highly recommend, if you have not done so already, that you take a class on Adobe Photoshop and basic HTML coding so that you can make your Wordpress and other web endeavors as beautiful and painless as possible. If you really wish to be brave, learn Java scripting also!

M. Nicole van Dam, in addition to exploring Facebook, works in many media, such as oils, acrylics, water color, pastels, pen and ink, and silk. In each work, one can find a passionate celebration of nature's beauty and diversity, which is Nicole's primary inspiration.

Nicole, a California native born of Dutch immigrant parents, was educated on the East Coast and is now living by California's Central Coast with her much-loved husband, dogs and bird.

Nicole writes about her artistic endeavors, pets and vegetable garden at her news blog, Wishes.bz. Nicole's parents are a tremendously positive influence in her life, and she attributes much of her success and love of the arts to them.

As a California native born of Dutch immigrant parents and educated in the East, Nicole's work expresses strong West Coast, East Coast, and European influences, artistically blended with Nicole's unique Impressionist flair. Nicole's style and distinctive color palette gives each work a new feel which is joyously whimsical, and yet somehow also reminiscent of a time when life was less hectic.

Creating engaging works that inspire, enchant and cheer, Nicole has been forging her own unique niche in the art world, earning excellent reviews and various one-man shows. Nicole is also an internationally licensed artist/designer, as well as a published poet and author of adult and children's books. An example of a children's book that she wrote and illustrated is "Inca Dink, the Great Houndini" (please see www.IncaDink.com to learn more). She also authored "Tempo –The Rhythm and Rhyme of the Artist" – a fun and inspirational book for adults blending art, poetry and philosophy.

Dedication

This Book is Dedicated to my patient husband, Jay, and my two dogs and birds, who make me laugh.

Other Books by M. Nicole van Dam:

SuperQuick ™ Facebook

Tempo – The Rhythm and Rhyme of the Artist

M. Nicole van Dam, a Retrospective 2010

Inca Dink, The Great Houndini

The Background Story of Inca Dink, The Great Houndini

To learn more, please visit Nicole.bz

Gondolier of Venice ™

An example of a painting by M. Nicole van Dam.

About the Cover Art: *"Rat Race™" is a painting by M. Nicole van Dam.*

All artwork used under license and © and TM M. Nicole van Dam. Learn more about this art at Nicole.bz

www.ingramcontent.com/pod-product-compliance
Lightning Source LLC
Chambersburg PA
CBHW041446210326
41599CB00004B/155